MY EDUCATED LIFE
lessons from leading schools
Paul Halford

PEDAGOGUE PUBLISHING

Copyright © **2025 Paul Halford.** All rights reserved.

PEDAGOGUE Publishing

First edition published 2025

Print ISBN: 978-1-8381361-5-4; EBook: 978-1-8381361-6-1

No parts of this publication may be reproduced, stored in a retrieval system, or transmitted in any form or by anymeans, electronic, mechanical, photocopying, recording, or otherwise, without the prior written permission of the copyright owner.

This book is sold subject to the condition that it shall not, by way of trade or otherwise, be lent, resold, hired out, or otherwise circulated without the publisher's prior consent in any form of binding or cover other than that in which it is published and without a similar condition including this condition being imposed on the subsequent purchaser. Under no circumstances may any part of this book be photocopied for resale.

This information contained within this book does not constitute legal or other professional advice; it cannot hope to offer all information available on the many themes covered. No liability is assumed for losses or damages due to the information provided. You are responsible for your own choices, actions, and results. Use your commonsense, do your own research and, if it all goes wrong, don't blame the book. Paul has provided the best advice he can based on his educated life, but it's only advice, and it's *his* life, not yours. Use the advice herein to inform your choices, but they are *your* choices.

Used sparingly, quotes are included and reproduced on the basis of 'fair use'; references direct readers to the original source, via which Paul hopes any copyright holders work will benefit.There is no intention to pass other works off as original to this text.

Edited by: Dr Denry Machin

Proof Reading: Nawal Kalra

For enquires regarding this book, or to publish with us, please contact: **admin@pedagogue.ac**

CONTENTS

Chapter		1
AN EDUCATED LIFE		2
About the Author		
1.	IN THE BEGINNING	4
	Hoi An, Vietnam	
2.	REIMAGINING SCHOOLS	8
	And Why We Need To Reimagine Them	
3.	CHANGE AND REIMAGINING	24
4.	PLANNING A REIMAGINING	39
5.	LEADING THE REIMAGINING	54
6.	PERFORMANCE MANAGEMENT AN ACT OF (RE)IMAGINATION	63
7.	TEACHERS	78
8.	PRINCIPALS	93
9.	CRISIS	106
	Dealing With The Things We Never Imagined	
10.	SAFE SCHOOLS	119

11.	SCHOOLS AND TECHNOLOGY	131
12.	REIMAGINING SCHOOLS - REVISTED	142
13.	AND IN THE END	160
	Lessons From A Life Lived in Education	

Dedicated to all the teachers along the way who were committed to the work.

Acknowledgements are offered to:

Peter Lanyon, Vic Branson, and Dr Denry Machin.

AN EDUCATED LIFE
About the Author

Twice nominated for a *National Excellence Award* (Australia), Paul has worked in education for nearly fifty years. Thirty-five of these have been in leadership. His 'educated life' is uniquely diverse, spanning Catholic, Jewish, Anglican, Islamic, government, international, and alternative schools.

In 1984 he was appointed to his first leadership position as the Principal of *The Kalang School*. Situated in a remote Australian valley, the school was owned and operated by the community. It was a pioneer in 'alternative' education. He held this position for ten years. In 1994 he accepted his first international position as the Principal of *Makassar International School* in Sulawesi, Indonesia. MIS was a small school serving the children of foreign NGO employees.

He returned to Australia in 1997 as Head of the Primary School at a large Anglican college. With an enrolment of over 1,200, the College became a leader in regional education. In 2003 and 2005 the school received national and state awards recognising its achievements in raising student standards through its professional development program.

After ten years' service to the College, in 2009 Paul accepted the position of Principal of *Korobosea International School*, Papua New Guinea. With an enrolment of 800 the school is one of the country's leading schools, one of twenty schools owned and operated by the *International Education Agency* of Papua New Guinea. In addition to his role as Principal, Paul was also a member of the Senior Leadership Council. This group had responsibility for policy development, school reviews and the mentoring of junior Principals.

In 2015 he was appointed Principal of two 'for-profit' schools in Malaysia. One of the schools, located in Kuala Lumpur had an enrolment of 850 students and the school in Johor Bahru, 300. Paul's time was divided between the two schools – and 350 kms. In 2017 Paul accepted the position of Foundation Principal of *Destiny International* in Muar, Malaysia. He was responsible for the school's transition from national to full international status. It was during this time that he was approached to assist other schools. This eventually became a consultancy. He also worked as a Link Tutor for *Warwick University's* PGCEi course.

Paul now lives in Hoi An in central Vietnam, with his wife, Van and daughter Nhim. He writes and records original music. He spends too much time on *Netflix*, reads the *Guardian* every morning while drinking strong black coffee and, with increasing exasperation, supports *Manchester United*.

IN THE BEGINNING
Hoi An, Vietnam

As I sit at my desk, writing these words, I am drawn to the view beyond it. The *Thu Bon River* glides towards the great, big world. I have been blessed to see much of that great, big world. Wanderlust—the urge to experience life on our extraordinary planet—has motivated me for over half a century of travel and adventure, much of it connected to schools. Now, as I slip into retirement, I have been given an opportunity to share these experiences.

We begin at the end. The end of a life lived in education.

Those experiences include attempted abductions (yes, of me), bus hijackings, library fires and, when I wasn't being held at knife point, thousands of delightful students and hundreds of dedicated teachers.

My journey covered seven schools in four countries, schools as varied as the countries they were in. They included a parent-operated community school in Australia, a not-for-profit international school in Indonesia, an award-winning Anglican college, a school that educated the national leadership of Papua New Guinea, for-profit and not-for-profit schools in Malaysia, and a consultancy in Vietnam. Each chapter of '*My Educated Life*' begins and ends with vignettes about these places. Travel and pedagogy are combined with cautionary tales, highlights, lowlights, and more than a few adventures along the way.

Welcome then to '*My Educated Life*.'

The words within are for those in school leadership and those aspiring to it. My intention is to provide you with practical advice distilled from my own thirty-five years in school leadership. An appointment to a position of leadership is a statement of belief by a school Board or owner. A belief that you are the right person to provide the three foundational values necessary for their school's success: **trust, hope,** and **care**.

> The Board/owner places its **trust** in you. You are the person to make their school successful. They have decided to trust your judgement—the key to leadership. You, in turn, will need to cultivate trust throughout the organisation. Trust is essential for success.
>
> The Board/owner expects you to **care** for its community. You will care about every student, and each staff member. You will also care about the school's reputation—you will preserve and enhance it. Care is the second pillar of success.
>
> Finally, the Board/owner places their **hope** in you. Their hope is that the school will improve under your stewardship. This hope is tacit permission for you to *reimagine* the school, to change it for the better. This is the great challenge of school leadership—to turn hopes, reimaginings, into reality.

Reimagining is the central theme of this book. We need to reimagine our classrooms, and schools. We need reimaginings both great and small. We need reimaginings because they create hope—hope that we can improve our schools.

With this book as a guide, your appointment as a school leader is an opportunity for you to become the *'reimaginer-in-chief'*.

An Overview of 'My Educated Life'

The book follows the chronological order of my appointments. Some of the geography, history, and culture of the countries I've worked in is provided. However, the chapters need not be read chronologically. You can 'drop-in' to any chapter.

We begin by looking at a UNESCO report from 2000 that provided six future scenarios for schools. The scenarios' origins are drawn from reimaginings created in the 1960s. A decade that saw the emergence of disruptors like AS Neill, Ivan Illich, John Holt, Lev Vygotsky and BF Skinner. As we'll see, each was influential in changing schools and education—and me. Chapters 3 to 6 offer practical advice for your own reimagining. There are chapters on change management, strategic planning, and performance management. These chapters reflect the legacy of a different group of disruptors: Fullan, Hargreaves, Hattie, Spady, and Robinson. Throughout the 1990's these new influencers led 'evidence based' reforms which still inform schools today.

Following this, Chapter 7 considers the teacher recruitment and retention crisis. What are the issues? What solutions might we provide? Chapter 8 focuses on the situation for

Principals. We look at the contradictions in the role and the various leadership styles Principals might adopt. In Chapters 9, 10 and 11 we look at the contemporary issues presented by technology, safeguarding, and critical incidents. Again, practical advice is offered to assist you in managing these challenges. In the penultimate chapter we return to the UNESCO report from Chapter 2, considering its predictions from our current situation. What relevance does it have today? Can these be a springboard for new reimaginings?

Regardless of the chapter's subject I emphasise throughout the importance of those three critical assets that every school needs: **trust**, **hope** and **care**. Each is necessary if our reimaginings are to become a reality. My modest hope is that '*My Educated Life*' will provide you with some directions, some solace, and some wisdom to help you realise your own reimaginings—to help you as you navigate your own 'educated life'.

Let's begin then at the beginning…in the remote Kalang Valley, Australia, where I took my first steps into school leadership.

REIMAGINING SCHOOLS
And Why We Need To Reimagine Them

"The goal of education should be creating men and women who are capable of doing things, not simply repeating what other generations have done"

Jean Piaget

Spend any time on social media, or watching the news, and you'll know that many parents and teachers are dissatisfied with schools. If you are a parent, teacher, or educator then your coffee shop conversations probably include the state of schools—and it probably isn't (always) positive.

A reimagining is needed. Of schools, and of the education system as a whole.

This chapter is a tour of some previous reimaginings: an introduction to disruptive educational thinkers whose influence endures today. It's a long chapter and for many readers perhaps a reminder of things studied during teacher training. Feel free to skim it, though it does set-up important context for the rest of the book. My hope is that this historical perspective might provide you with some inspiration for your own reimagining—whether that's of your own school, your own children's education, your own teaching, or of the system within which you work.

My Educated Life

Kalang Valley, Australia, 1984-1994

My first leadership appointment was as Principal of the *Kalang Community School*. It would challenge my assumptions about schools, teaching, and learning.

Situated 500 kms north of Sydney, the Kalang Valley nestles in the foothills of the Great Dividing Range that separates coastal Australia from its vast interior. Kalang had initially been cleared by 'soldier-settlers' following the First World War. Veterans were provided with small acreages in recognition of their service. However, the lush rainforest greenery was deceptive. The topsoil was thin and unsuitable for crops or animals. The soldier-settlers fought on but by the early 1960s, most were gone, exhausted by a different kind of battle.

Then, in the early 1970s, a new wave of settlers began to adopt the valley as their home. It was a reimagining that led my wife and I to build a house on a small plateau, one hundred metres above the valley floor. We intended to "live simply so that others can simply live". We attempted to reduce our 'footprint' decades before it became a climatic necessity. We used the first generation of solar panels for electricity and water from rain tanks. It was a rewarding but demanding life.

The school I was appointed to lead was the centre of the community. It had been built by parents who were resolute in maintaining its independence from

> government funding and oversight. We didn't follow the national curriculum nor any specific pedagogy. We created an independent school that produced well-balanced and productive graduates. One became a star of the *Moscow State Circus*, another founded his own tech company, one pioneered outdoor education in remote schools, another opened a chain of gyms.
>
> The single most important characteristic of *Kalang School* graduates was not their grades but their confidence. It was my introduction to schooling 'reimagined'.

Why We Need To Reimagine Schools

How many parents have sat at the dinner table and asked their child:

"What did you learn in school today?"

And received the dismissive reply:

"Nothing"

Too many. Too many schools are not realising the incredible potential of the children enrolled within them.

This is why we need to reimagine schooling.

Anybody familiar with the daily life of a three-year old will smile while recollecting their imaginative play, their creative freedom, their curiosity (the inexhaustible *"whys?"*), and their unique self-expression. Yet, when these same children begin schooling, and become 'schooled', these natural inclinations are all too often subsumed.

This is why we need to reimagine schooling.

For many children, schools are not working. We are failing to provide environments that nurture the best in our children. It is not the teachers' or the Principals' or the government's fault. We simply have outgrown the institution. It is struggling to remake itself into a new and more relevant form.

This is why we need to reimagine schooling.

Consider this hypothetical: A suburban high school has been closed due to falling enrolments. The local education authority decides to sell the site. Which other industry could repurpose the school without significant outlay? For their money, a developer would get:

- Perimeter walls designed to keep people in (and out); access control on doors.
- Bells and PA systems to direct movements.
- Uniformly designed spaces (classrooms), easily converted to alternative use.
- Recreational spaces and sports facilities; a canteen and dining area/s.
- Vocational training spaces (Design & Technology labs etc).
- Reasonable parking; sufficient toilets for a thousand people.
- Separate administration areas, with extra security provisions and capacity for a full lockdown.

What comes to mind? A hospital perhaps. Or maybe a jail. Which is exactly what happened. The situation is not a hypothetical. A few years back a US high school was sold to a company providing low-security penitentiaries. They got a ready-made prison.

This is why we need to reimagine schooling.

Imagining The Schools Of The Future

In 2000 UNESCO published a paper predicting six possible scenarios for schools in the future[1].

- In the **first scenario**, schools continue to muddle through with increasing dissatisfaction and bureaucracy (at the time of writing, that sounds familiar).

- In the **second scenario**, schools become profit centres—often part of a corporate structure.

- In the **third scenario**, focus shifts to the emotional and social welfare of students.

- In the **fourth**, schools become vibrant learning communities with a strong academic focus.

- In the **fifth scenario**, schools are replaced by individual learning networks which do not need a physical setting or predetermined hours.

- In the **final scenario**, teacher scarcity causes the widespread closure of schools.

---

1. World Education Report. UNESCO 2000

It is instructive to review these projections from our current position. They seem very prescient; and, in Chapter 12 we'll return to these scenarios, considering each in contemporary light. For now, it's worth noting that Scenarios 2, 3, 4 and 5 have their roots in the reimagining of schools provided by influencers from previous generations. Which is where we now head.

The Influencers

Assumptions about human nature are the starting point for any reimagining of education. Other assumptions regarding the purpose of education, the nature of knowledge, and the implications for classroom practice follow and flow from it.

Human nature is also the starting point for historical influencers who reimagined schooling.

The late 1960s were changing times in education. The 'alternative school' movement was at the front of broader educational reforms. The impact of educators who challenged the moribund nature of schools was increasingly significant. There were 'influencers' like AS Neill and Summerhill School where there were no rules governing behaviour but an expectation that students could self-regulate. Ivan Illich argued for the deschooling of society. Lev Vygotsky's work was in translation. John Holt was sitting in the back of New York classrooms—an anthropologist of modern culture—that culminated in his inspiring 'Why Children Fail.'

But before all of these was 'Emile'.

Human Nature

Seventeenth century Jean Jacques Rousseau's imaginary education of a young French aristocrat raised the fundamental question of education: 'What is human nature?' For Rousseau:

> "Everything is good as it leaves the hands of the Author of things, everything degenerates in the hands of man." [2]

This view of human nature had a lot of traction in the alternative school movement in countries as diverse as Turkey, the US, France, South Africa, and the UK. The parents and teachers in these schools sought to provide an educational environment built on the assumption that human nature was good and needed to be preserved.

REFLECTION

On childhood and schooling: As a parent, how do/did you view your child's first few years?
On human nature: Are we born 'good' and spoiled by society?
As a teacher: What are your assumptions about human nature?
And, combined: What are the implications of these assumptions for your own philosophy of education?

A.S. Neill and the Alternative School Movement

The third UNESCO scenario predicts schools that are primarily focused on student wellbeing and emotional development. *Summerhill* is one of those schools.

Founded 100 years ago in an English manor house, *Summerhill* was one of the first schools to place wellbeing at the centre of its pedagogy. Its founder A.S. Neill was determined to create a school which respected the rights of students and sought to develop their full potential. Neill had a fierce belief in the goodness of human nature and the need for it to be preserved. Students chose whether to attend lessons and how they would live — without imposing on others. *Summerhill*'s website self-describes the school as a 'free range' environment.

At *Summerhill* each student's wellbeing was respected and recognised decades before the term became popular. Academic achievement is subordinate to emotional development. Neill believed that once a student's social/emotional needs were met they would naturally turn to learning and academics.

Neill's Legacy

Neill died in 1973 but *Summerhill* continues to this day.

His legacy is much more than the school. Neill's beliefs have influenced thousands of educators. The alternative practices developed (sometimes successfully, sometimes less so) in these schools have had a major influence on mainstream schooling. Much of what we now take for granted as 'best practice' has its genesis in these schools. For example:

- Child-centred education (I know, it's impossible to imagine it wasn't ever thus, but...it wasn't)

- Active and Discovery Learning

- Parent partnerships in education/with educators

- Integrated Units of Learning

- Collaborative Planning

- Pastoral care (again...hard to imagine it wasn't always a priority)

The alternative school movement has not disappeared. It manifests itself today in the popular *Steiner* and *Montessori* methodologies. The *Reggio Emilia* movement is another form of reimagined education. Perhaps the most intriguing contemporary manifestation of the alternative school is the '*Think Global School*', a travelling high school which sets up in a different part of the world each term. The visionaries behind *Think* want the students to get 'real world explanations'. In 2024 the school was set up in Canada, moved to Brazil, went onto Vietnam, and finally to Italy. It is unashamedly idealistic.

These schools are the latest manifestations of a movement to change education through radical reimagination rather than incremental steps. Yet, they remain niche. We still have walls, of all types. They have influenced thinking but have not triggered radical, system-wide transformation. But, I remain hopeful. I place some of that hope in systems like the *International Baccalaureate*.

> **REFLECTION**
>
> **On alternative thinking:** How many of the practices listed above, or used by *Summerhill*, are currently used in your school? Could any be introduced?
>
> **On disruption:** Neill was a disruptor. Is the role of a school leader to disrupt or to provide stability and surety? Or is the role about introducing and managing change?

The International Baccalaureate

A more recent example of reimagining, and perhaps one more familiar to you, is the *International Baccalaureate* (IB).

In the 1960s international schooling was not the global industry it is today[3]. Most international schools would implement the national curriculum of their home country, but from 1968 an increasing number began to adopt the International Baccalaureate. Today, there are over 5,000 IB schools, educating 2 million students.

Echoing the fourth UNESCO scenario, the IB is an extraordinary achievement. It is a curriculum created by educators for educators. For the IB, the how is more important than the what and when. Per UNESCO, the IB creates strong learning communities with vibrant pedagogy and high academic expectations.

---

3. For those interested in international schooling I recommended '*International Schooling: The Teacher's Guide*' by Dr Denry Machin and Dr Stephen Whitehead. It covers the history and development of these schools, offers careers advice, and job hunting tips.

As a contrast, I have had responsibility for school registrations in Australia, Papua New Guinea and Malaysia. This involved teams of inspectors visiting the school. Their primary focus was always what we were teaching and when. The IB accreditation inspections are different. They are all about the how—how the teaching and the learning is being conducted. IB inspectors spend a lot of time in classrooms observing what's actually happening.

The IB is unashamedly internationalist. In the mid 1960s, this was revolutionary. The primary purpose of schooling up to that point was to create national unity. The nation's youth would salute the flag and sing the national anthem in assemblies. They would study the nation's history and learn the nation's language. The knowledge, skills, and values of the curriculum would be purposed to nation building. The IB program offered a radically different reimagining.

Deschooling Society

The most radical reimagining of schools to emerge from the 1960s was Ivan Illich's argument that we should abolish schools altogether. A wish many readers have perhaps shared!

Illich was a priest and social activist. He was critical of society's institutional approach to education, an approach that constrains learning to specific times and places—to schools. He argued for self-directed education based on informal arrangements, which he called 'education webs'. This is the fifth UNESCO prediction: personalised education happening outside of schools, no longer confined to a specific place or time.

Illich's 'Deschooling Society' was visionary. It predicted a proliferation of 'learning networks', with computers connecting learners with educators. This was decades before the explosion of the internet. Illich imagined a pluralistic, decentralised, and freedom-based learning environment. His reimagining has become a twenty-first century reality. Learning can take place in cafes, at home, and on park benches. Learners can (and during COVID, were) freed from the many restrictions imposed by schools.

Of all the reimaginings to emerge from the late 1960s Illich's was the most radical but also the most prescient. His educational philosophy blended technology, pedagogy, and theology to produce a compelling argument for self-directed, lifelong learners who were not restricted by institutional limitations—a vision now being realised by AI.

Schools Reimagined as Profit Centres

UNESCO's second scenario predicts schools as profit-centres either as private fee-paying schools or as part of a corporation in which education might be only one of the business's income streams.

This 'businessing' of education is in full swing. Schools are now unquestionably businesses, even those run by the State. Parents are customers, students are clients. The bottom line is that the bottom-line matters. This is especially true in international schools—and particularly so in Asia.

In the late 1990s governments throughout the world repealed regulations prohibiting their nationals from enrolling in international schools. It opened a floodgate. The change in regulations brought about a massive increase in the number of international schools—mostly created by local businesspeople eyeing a lucrative new market. A lot of teaching jobs were created, and a lot of money was to be made.

The primary purpose of these schools is to make profit; a reimagining driven by finance as much as by education. Up to the point of deregulation most independent schools were 'not-for-profit'. Any surplus would be reinvested for the benefit of the school community. In contrast, the owners of 'for-profit' schools determine the level of reinvestment mindful of investors' expectations of a financial return. The primacy of the 'mission' that we as educators place on schools might not be shared by the owners. For many of these owners their schools are often only one part of their business activity and often not the primary focus. They are likely to have construction, retail, or manufacturing in their portfolios as well. Schools are just another 'product', another profit line.

This reimagining of schools is fraught with contradictions and tensions. The leadership of these schools must navigate the tension between the expectation of minimising costs with the expectation of strong academic results. Machin asks:

> "what happens to schools [and] school leaders...where the school's raison d'etre, is no longer solely educational? Can Heads retain credibility as educational specialists...while achieving primary tasks that are commercially orientated?" [4]

---

4. Machin, D (2019) The Organisational Evolution of Contemporary International Schools, Journal of Research in International Education, p110.

One of the most profound changes with fee-paying schools is in the relationship between teachers and parents. Teachers became 'providers' and parents became 'clients' or 'customers.' It was a change that triggered several responses. Parents' expectations of the school and their children increased. Parents saw their child's enrolment as a form of contract. School leaders became cautious in dealing with student behaviour lest it result in a withdrawal and loss of income.

> **REFLECTION**
>
> **On for-profit education:** Can for-profit schools provide quality education?
> **On leading for-profit schools:** How would you manage, both day-to-day and in terms of your own educational philosophy, the (potential) contradiction between profit and educational quality?

Professor Skinner and the Learning Machines

The final reimagining from the 1960s to consider was provided by an American academic, B. F. Skinner.

Skinner was a behavioural psychologist. He predicted that 'learning machines' would replace teachers for the delivery of education. He believed that behaviour is developed (or conditioned) through reinforcement. He referred to this process as operant conditioning, with operant referring to any behaviour that acts on the environment and leads to consequences. Skinner argued that the response or reinforcement could be provided more effectively by computers than by classroom teachers.

For Skinner, computers can more effectively teach skills and knowledge because of shorter feedback loops. The closer the response is to the action the more effective the conditioning. A teacher might take minutes or days to give feedback, a computer less than a second. Skinner argued that machine-based learning would allow the student to work at their own pace—an early expression of adaptive teaching (differentiation).

In this reimagining, aligned with UNESCO's fifth scenario, the role of teachers is reduced to socialisation.

My Educated Life

> *Kalang Valley, Australia*
>
> This chapter began in a small school in a remote valley in northern New South Wales. The *Kalang School* was an alternative school and my own introduction to schooling 'reimagined'. It drew inspiration from A.S. Neill's Summerhill. Students' social/emotional development was the primary purpose; parents were relaxed about academic achievements.
>
> The community believed that the rearing of children was everyone's responsibility.
>
> They do say it takes a village to raise a child.

Over the course of this chapter, I have outlined the ideas and influence of educators who reimagined schools. Which of the reimaginings are you most attracted to? And what assumptions about human nature do you have?

Which reimaginings might provide, or point to, solutions to the existing problems schools are facing? Problems of teacher recruitment and retention? Problems of an emerging school leadership vacuum? Problems of student engagement? Problems of resource levels? Problems of curriculum relevancy? And so on.

Your answers depend, of course, on whether you see yourself as a *guardian* or an *influencer*. Will you be an inspiration for the next reimagining: of your own school, of your own children's education, of your own teaching, or of the system within which you work?

CHANGE AND REIMAGINING

"Our dilemma is that we hate change and love it at the same time; what we really want is for things to remain the same but get better."

Sydney J. Harris

In this third chapter we consider how any reimagining of schools must invoke change—and the management of change.

Managing change is one of the most demanding aspects of leadership. The first tasks are to identify the need for change, establish the direction of the change, and then to develop a plan to introduce the change. The second and much more difficult challenge is the actual implementation. This challenge can be moderated by **trust, care**, and **hope**—those three critical assets in managing change. As I'll describe, you should also expect resistance to change; especially if the reimagining deviates from school 'norms'.

My Educated Life

Makassar South Sulawesi, Indonesia, 1994-97

My second leadership appointment was on the Indonesian island of Sulawesi and its capital Makassar. We were provided with a pleasant house in Mango Street, bought a boat called 'Sunday' and spent weekends exploring nearby coral islands. We played baseball with Japanese parents. As a family, it was the best of times.

Makassar is known for its ethnic people—the Bugis. Infamous as pirates, the origin of the 'bogey man' is from the Dutch fear of the Bugis pirates. Though piracy isn't the only reason for their fame. Anyone who visited Singapore in the 1960s to 1980s would have likely included a visit to Bugis Street. People came to see (and marvel) at the transgender women sashaying along the street. But, the story of Indonesia's trans Bugis is much more poignant than a tourist trap. In traditional Bugis society there were five genders, consistent with the view that gender existed on a spectrum. The fifth of these, the Bissu, were revered religious leaders, intermediaries between people and Gods. All this changed with the Dutch colonial administration and then Suharto's New Order. Most of the transgender women parading in Bugis Street were exiles from Makassar.

Change comes in many forms, not always good.

The Book of Change and Reimagining

It is a common reaction, in times of need, for people to turn to their 'Good Book' for inspiration, solace, and guidance. For centuries the Bible, the Quran, and the Vedas have been supporting human beings in their struggle to make sense of life. I have a 'bible' too. It is Michael Fullan's *'New Meaning of Educational Change'*. I have been reading and absorbing this book for over thirty years. I once heard Fullan referred to as "St Michael of Toronto", but that is probably pushing the theology too far.

I am not alone in this adoration. Consider this review by Diana Watson, the Director of Professional Development for the Centre of School Success, in New Hampshire:

> "I take it everywhere I go. I keep snatching it up and opening to one of the many sticky-noted pages to quote a pertinent paragraph. Frankly, I wish I could memorise the entire book."[1]

My copy is the second edition and the third reprint. There have been four editions and ten reprints! This is 384 pages of demanding reading. The large number of reprints is an indication of the high regard educators around the world have for it.

My initial encounter with *'The New Meaning of Educational Change'* coincided with my second appointment as a school Principal. I read the sections on Change, Teachers, and Principals avidly. I read it on planes, I read it while waiting

---

1. Watson D (2008) 'Connections', *Journal of National School Reform*, Winter, p1

for junior basketball games to start, and I read it in the early hours whilst working on my Master's degree. It has guided me in my reimagining of schools.

It is fundamental to Fullan that school managers understand the nature of change and what is required to achieve successful change. Fullan writes that the most important thing is "*a feel for the change process*". As we'll explore below, it is important to note Fullan's choice of the word '*feel*'. Managing change is as much art as administration[2].

Sitting alongside 'feel', Fullan insists upon the importance of communication in achieving successful change. For Fullan frequent and personal interactions are the key to implementation. His research revealed that educational leaders' work time is dominated by interactions. He writes:

> "The effective administrator is one who constantly works at communication because difficulties in communication are natural and inevitable".[3]

And, of course, all change is based in that most artful of human endeavours – relationships. Fullan emphasises the place and importance of personal relationships in achieving sustainable change. It is in the exchange of understanding about a change that the chances of successful implementation lie. A Principal or a system supervisor might well see the importance and merit of a change. They might

---

2. Fullan M (1991) "The New Meaning of Educational Change" Continuum, London, p5

3. Ibid, P200

communicate the change articulately. They might provide training and resources. However, it is unlikely to lead to sustained school or system-wide change unless the people implementing it are given the opportunity to clarify, to complain, and to collaborate about the change. This will require strong relationships that can weather dissent.

Pressure and Support

One of the most challenging aspects of change leadership is to balance the contradictory forces of **support** and **pressure**—of encouraging and coercing. Fullan specifically nominates the orchestration of "*pressure and support*" as necessary for school improvement:

> "It is so difficult to get change started and so easy to see it stopped." [4]

In other words, sometimes pressure is needed to maintain momentum.

Core to successfully implementing change is managing this contradiction of support and pressure. In a good relationship the leader builds 'social capital' with the staff. The leader is someone who can be trusted, who is authoritative, but who also cares. They'll coach and guide. They'll fix people's problems. They'll support. At the same time, they'll also push. They'll lean on social capital to drive change. With enough social capital, staff will (to some extent) suspend their doubts, trusting that a change is not just another misguided or under-resourced idea, but something that might prove

---

4. Ibid, P210

beneficial. Or, at the very least, they won't (overly and overtly) resist the pressure to change.

> Fullan reminds us that:
> ⊠⊠Change is a subjective experience.
> ⊠⊠Constant communication about a change is essential.
> ⊠⊠Managing change requires support and pressure.
> ⊠⊠The quality of the relationship between leader and staff will affect implementation.

Ralph Stacey and the Mediators

I first saw the '*Stacey Diagram*' at a Principals' conference in Adelaide. It is remarkably effective in explaining the requirements for successful change management. Stacey argues that any change will involve a loss of surety and agreement. Take, for example, changes to a school's daily timetable. There will be a period of transition. It is in the transition that surety and agreement are at risk. If the transition is not managed effectively it can lead to chaos. The result can be an abandonment of the initiative and a retreat to the surety and agreement that operated previously.

Echoing many of Fullan's comments, Stacey argues that there are mediators to manage the transition. These are:

- Trust
- Communication
- A shared sense of mission
- Not blaming others

- Accepting responsibility

If there is one learning I took away from reading Fullan and Stacey, it is that change is a subjective experience. Objective planning and logical arguments for a change will not assuage the subjective feelings it incites in those being expected to change. It arouses feelings. Feelings of anxiety or inadequacy. Perhaps feelings of resentment and suspicion. These feelings might be expressed openly or whispered in corridors.

If you want your change to succeed, you will need to hear these voices.

A leader's best resource in managing change is the trust that the staff have in them. The staff are more likely to suspend their doubts and accept any additional work if they have sufficient belief in their leader's judgement. This 'social capital' is built on leaders providing the three resources essential to leading change: trust, hope, and care.

> **REFLECTION**
> **On Change:** Are you comfortable with change? Or do you prefer stability?
> **On Pressure and Support:** Are they contradictory or complementary? What drives leaders to exert pressure?
> **On Loss of Surety:** Does change erode agreements?
> **On Subjectivity:** How can we reduce the disturbance that change brings?

Trust, Hope and Care

It is hopefully clear by now that, for me at least, three resources are essential to the successful reimagining of a school. A school can have the best equipment, the finest facilities, and the highest speed internet; however, it all counts for little if these three fundamental resources are absent. Trust, hope and care are essential to leading and achieving a reimagining.

Trust

Leaders must cultivate trust. You build trust by delivering on your promises, by listening to your people's concerns and by taking an interest in their lives outside the workplace. Teachers who trust their leader will be willing to support decisions on new programs and even reimaginings. You gain trust by bending the rules, by tweaking the system, and by taking a genuine interest in people. In turn, when you need the staff's trust in your judgement, you are likely to receive it.

Bryk and Schneider's study of 'trust levels' found that schools with high levels of relational trust were "three times more likely to be categorised as improving in reading and maths" than those with low levels of trust. They also found:

> "...the most telling data showed that schools with weak trust had virtually no chance of showing improvement".[5]

Hope

The best gift we can give staff in schools is hope. Hope that it is worth coming to work, hope that workloads will become

---

5. Browning P (2013) "Creating the Conditions for Transformational Change", AEL Vol 35, Number 3, p15

manageable, and hope that things will change for the better. Hope that reimagining will improve the situation.

Without hope that a school will change for the better, staff become cynical. A black humour becomes embedded in the culture. Such humour might help teachers get through their day, but it has an insidious effect on their wellbeing. Without hope a toxic culture can develop. Teaching becomes unpleasant and unrewarding.

In one school I inspected there had been a succession of Principals. One had lasted a term, another a year. All had left following disagreements with the proprietor of this privately owned school. One of the most concerning aspects of this turnover in leadership was the way it had drained hope from the teachers. It did not matter how skilled or experienced the new Principal was, the staff no longer believed the new leader's enthusiasm and efforts would make any difference.

Care

The owner of another school I inspected complained that the teachers in the school "*just don't care.*" From observations, this appeared to be true. There were classes without teachers, behaviour was unmanaged, teachers did not attend their duties, and lesson planning was rudimentary. "*Why don't they care?*" was the owner's complaint.

The simple answer was that they did not feel cared about. Their employment contract created indentured labour, they were never thanked for their efforts. Any absent days resulted in loss of wages regardless of the circumstances. The staff did not feel valued or cared for. In turn they cared little about their work or their students.

Leaders must demonstrate that they care about and are willing to listen to their staff's needs and opinions.

> **REFLECTION**
> **On Trust, Hope and Care:** Are you confident that you can provide these three resources? Can you think of any examples in your daily practice?

Resisting the Reimagining

Many people dislike change. Some people hate change. Change creates uncertainty and uncertainty raises feelings. Feelings of frustration that yet another change is being introduced. Feelings of inadequacy as the implementation dip begins. Feelings of ambiguity about the worth of the change. None of these are welcome feelings.

Change upsets the stability of the existing order. We should anticipate resistance to change because of the feelings it provokes, because, however objective the reasons for change, what matters most are the subjective experiences of those expected to change. The resistance can come in various forms:

- It might be unconscious.
- It might be wilful refusal.
- It might be passive evasion.
- It might be specific, or it could be generalised.
- It might be non-compliance.
- It might be compelling counter arguments.

It is predictable but difficult to plan for subjective resistance. We should not underestimate an organisation's capacity to protect itself.

It is also important that the authors of the change do not have their own subjective reactions to the resistance. As staff criticise, dismiss, and even belittle a proposal, it is all too easy for the author's own subjective feelings to surface. It's a very human process.

My advice: see change as a collaborative process. In a collaboration you hear other voices, other points of view, and can work towards an agreed goal. You value their contributions enough to let their contributions reshape the change where it is warranted. This requires flexibility. It requires trust, care, and hope. The implementation phase will also demand adjustments and adaptations—changes to the change that the author of the change might not be comfortable changing.

> **REFLECTION**
> **On Valuing Resistance:** Should we tolerate resistance or embrace it?
> **On Collaboration:** Are collaborative leaders always the most effective?

Escaping the Iron Cage

My morning walk takes me past a Vietnamese government school. They are usually holding their morning assembly. It is disturbing to see the similarities between this assembly and others I have witnessed around the world. The Deputy Principal speaks from a lectern about timetables and events. She invites the Principal to provide a homily. The students are arranged in classes around a quadrangle. Boys in the back rows chaff under the restraint of expected behaviour. A conscientious teacher chooses to patrol and control them. Other teachers ignore the behaviour engrossed in their own conversations. I doubt that any of the actors in the scene have been instructed in the form and behaviour expected. The scene conforms to 'norms' we would see at schools everywhere. These norms maintain the appearance of a 'legitimate' school—one doing what schools do.

The point? The reward for similarity is credibility.

Schools seek legitimacy in the eyes of the profession and the eyes of parents by being 'normal'. A school looks, sounds, and feels the way a school should, or how people imagine it should, because it follows the accepted norms. School legitimacy is not a product of reimaging but its opposite—conformity.

If we start to reimagine schools, when does a school stop being legitimate? When does a school stop doing what schools do and start doing, and being, something else? In its early years Summerhill's legitimacy as a school was questioned by education authorities, the media, and the general public. (See Chapter 2). Reimagining, doing things differently, is not without its risks.

It is not just the institutions but also the individuals within the institutions who maintain the impetus towards similarity. School leaders are also under pressure to conform to field norms. School leaders:

> "...not only shape [their] schools according to accepted norms, but also subsume their own selves to a professionally defined normative identity."[6]

This is not good news for the reimaginers.

Professional attire projects the expected appearance of a school leader. Fair enough, but it is not only appearance. The role sets boundaries on behaviour which shapes school leaders' lives well beyond the work environment. For example, a local lawyer intoxicated and swaying his way home will draw little commentary, but a school Principal observed in the same state would create a storm of community concern. The role requires stability and sobriety and Principals must bend themselves to the role.

How can a reimagining be achieved when the life force of the institution, and society's view of the institution, is the primary obstacle to change?

Machin argues that: "Individuals can change organisations in agentic and creative ways", because:

> "What is proper or appropriate organisational behaviour is open for (re)interpretation by school leaders imaginative enough and strong enough to break from the 'iron cage' of isomorphy."[7]

---

6. Op Cit, Machin, p110

7. Ibid, Machin, p110

We can bend ourselves to the role, or we can use the role to bend our schools to us. Michael Fullan uses the term 'cosmopolitans' to describe these types of leaders. We'll return to this in Chapter 8.

My Educated Life

Makassar, Indonesia

After three years in Makassar we loaded our belongings into a shipping container and said goodbye to Mango St.

How did this 'cosmopolitan' experience affect my own reimagining? *Makassar International* had been a melting pot of nations. Inclusion was a necessary condition for its viability—the immigrants, the neurodiverse, and those on the gender spectrum. The Bugis from the opening of this chapter did not 'tolerate' or 'accept' transgendered people—they valued them.

During my time in Makassar, I had lived in a city where for centuries five genders had co-existed. As a result, wherever I worked next, I knew that I wanted to see schools implementing 'inclusiveness'. Fast forward to today and most schools have reimagined diversity. It has been an important reimagining. It has not always been planned, but a plan certainly helps.

I suggest you build your own plan around those three words: **trust**, **hope**, and **care**.

My educated life has taught me that the most important aspect of managing change is to understand the subjective experience of the people charged with implementing the change. If we do not listen to, clarify, and collaborate with the people navigating the change we are likely to be disappointed in the result.

We have also to consider that resistance to change could be a result of the school's (necessary) need for legitimacy; legitimacy that is primarily achieved through conformity to industry norms not through change and reimagining.

Radicalism may need to be reined in.

Change may require baby steps.

In your own reimagining, whether of your department, school, or section, you may need to factor in how you can both reimagine and remain legitimate.

PLANNING A REIMAGINING

"When you plan for upcoming things, you are actually living in them. It is therapeutic to live in your dream but you also need to keep yourself in the reality."

Winston Churchill

In the second chapter I presented influential reimaginings of schools. Hopefully, they have inspired you to consider changes for your school. In the third chapter we looked at how to manage change and its importance to a successful reimagining. In the next three chapters I will present practical approaches for implementing a reimagining.

The approaches are complementary.

The first, this chapter, is the development of a strategic plan; the second chapter sees school leaders changing their schools through 'leading the learning' of the reimagining; the third uses performance management to help teachers perform their own act of (re)imagination.

My Educated Life

Coffs Harbour, New South Wales, Australia, 1998-2007

After the idyllic years in Makassar our return to Australia invoked no small amount of culture shock.

Culture shock will not only affect you when you move to a foreign destination but also on your return home. The re-entry requires a readjustment not only to how things were, but to what they have become. Friends and family have changed. The place may have changed. Your sense of the place will have changed. You've changed.

Inevitably then, my return to Australia required significant readjustment. Not least because my next home, Coffs Harbour, is quintessentially Australian. It is casual and egalitarian; facets of Australian life that Aussies take great pride in. 'Coffs' is a small city situated on the strip of land running along the east coast between the Pacific Ocean and the mountains of the Great Dividing Range. It has a sub-tropical climate, good air, and clean water. The beaches are magnificent and dominate the lives of the residents. The popular expression *"getting a fair go"* typifies the local belief that there should be equal opportunity for everyone.

Little surprise then that my new appointment as the Principal of the primary school in a private Anglican college was not without its challenges. It is fair to say that the establishment of a private college was viewed by many in Coffs Harbour as unwanted elitism. Nevertheless, the doors to the college opened in January 1994 with an initial enrolment of 44 Primary aged

> students. When I joined, enrolment had risen to 450, including Secondary students, but there was a sense that development was stalling.
>
> It needed some reimagining.

Strategic Planning

The school I now found myself in was…stuck. The previous Head of Primary had resigned after differences with the Headmaster. The teaching staff were divided between progressives and traditionalists. Enrolment targets were not being achieved. I decided that what was needed was a plan. A 'Strategic Plan'—data driven and evidence-based. These were big buzzwords in education in the late 90s.

Years earlier when working in construction, I had seen construction engineers undertake critical-path analysis. Critical paths set out timelines for each phase of a building project. Would a similar precise approach to planning work for a school improvement plan?

The short answer: **no**.

Why not? Well, the key difference is the raw materials. Engineers use steel and concrete. School leaders work with human beings. Engineers are usually implementing their plans on clear sites. Principals are implementing their plans in crowded (and busy) workplaces. The implementation of engineers' plans rarely impacts the values of the people charged with the implementation. Leaders in schools must navigate through the competing values of staff, owners, parents, and students.

As we explored in Chapter 3, balancing people's subjective experience of 'the change' and objective adherence to 'the plan' is key to successful implementation. Achieving change with people requires empathy and flexibility. Plans to change schools that are tightly scripted and require a high level of fidelity, like those of engineers, are unlikely to succeed. You cannot expect blind faith and unquestioned acceptance. Your plan will be subjected to scrutiny and critique – either openly or in whispered conversations.

So, with my first idea cast aside, what kind of plan was needed?

A chance meeting with the Principal of a successful school provided me with a solution. He gave me a template for a Strategic Plan. It was fortuitous because in the mid 1990s strategic planning in schools did not have the exposure it has today. Now, a simple *Google* search will provide multiple commercial versions and expertise. In the mid 1990s there was no *Google*.

The template I received provided for 'Priority Areas', each addressing a school need or concern identified by evidence. Critically, the evidence acted as benchmarks at the beginning and conclusion of the project. It would provide the measures of success – what we'd now call '*Key Performance Indicators* (KPIs)'. All very obvious today, but cutting-edge back then.

We should not be surprised though if our precious plans meet resistance. Sure, strategic planning should be based on evidence that convinces us of the necessity for a change. It should be logical and objective. Yet, even if it is logical and objective, that may matter little when the plan meets human emotions. Someone will object to the additional work involved, another will suggest something extra which isn't part of the plan, yet another will question the timeline. No doubt you've been there. No doubt you've had push-back on your own plans.

However well meant, this push-back can often be perceived as opposition and, as a leader, our first reaction might be *"No, that's not how we planned it"*. This impulse to reject and shut down alternative opinions, fighting for the purity of 'your' plan, will almost certainly create more resistance. If we want some level of staff acceptance and ownership it is most likely to come through dialogue—though it can be exhausting having to explain and defend yourself!

> **REFLECTION**
> **On Strategic Plans:** Can we plan logically for all issues in schools? How much flexibility around the plan should we provide? Do we need complete 'buy in?'

What Are the Elements of a 'Priority Area'?

A priority area is composed of elements that are intended to guide its implementation.

- The evidence that demonstrates the concern.
- A clearly stated goal.
- The evidence that will be used to measure the success of the initiative.
- Who will have responsibility for the priority?
- What strategies will be implemented?
- What is the implementation timeline?
- What costs are anticipated?

A sample of a simple Priority Area plan is provided below.

2025 Strategic Plan

Priority Area – Parent and Community Partnership

Goal: To improve the relationship between the teachers and the parents.
Evidence: Parent surveys; Teacher surveys; Student surveys; Anecdotal
Target: To raise survey scores by 0.3 on each item within two years.

	Staff	Time	Cost	Status
Maintain and develop Parent Education sessions to address mismatched expectations. (eg: parents view themselves as customers expecting service from the school)	Paul, Joseph	Monthly	Nil	On-going

---

This plan was successful. The teacher and parent survey results from the following years indicated that the relationship between the two groups had significantly improved. However, not all plans…go to plan.

The Challenges

In my experience there are several challenges that you will have to negotiate – often literally from day one.

The first challenge will be traction.

The initial week back after the long summer holiday is usually pupil free. It might seem like the ideal time to present your great and grand plan. However, the staff gathered around you might not share your focus. Your experienced senior teacher is fretting over a plan to coordinate her mother's home care. Your newly appointed first year teacher has worked assiduously for the last two weeks to prepare for the start of her career, but still feels like an imposter. Your Learning Support teacher did not get much sleep the night before due to their son's illness. Another staff member is calculating her mortgage repayments, again. This is the reality your plan lands in – the jumbled, emotional reality of the human condition. Getting people to focus on it, to start to get traction under it, will be your first challenge. Your teachers are likely to be focused on surviving the first week back.

A wise Head would curb their enthusiasm. In the chapter on Change I emphasised the importance of relationships in achieving change. The first few weeks of the new school year is probably not the time to push for major changes. It would be better to focus on trust, care, and hope – those three key resources. You might have to give your experienced teacher some time off, and trust she will not waste the time. Your new teacher might need a dose of hope that their workload will get easier. Your sleep deprived Learning Support teacher will benefit from some caring words. This is all a precursor to introducing the plan – timing – the art of leadership.

But timing can get complicated.

On that first day it is also likely that the school's annual calendar will be presented. The starter gun is fired. In my experience school calendars are already crowded with the hundred and one things that schools are expected to provide – day in day out. Parent evenings, school concerts, athletics carnivals, assessment periods, charity fundraisers, remembrance days, excursions, and national holidays will all reduce the focus on your plan, and the time available to implement it. You might get to the end of the year and wonder why so little of the plan was realised.

One solution that worked for me was to buy teachers' time. I looked at my budget and saw scope for savings that I channelled into release days for teachers. The teachers' participation in and implementation of the Strategic Plan was 'purchased'. Not an ideal solution but it did create the necessary initial traction.

Another challenge to your plan might come from the owner or Board. Owners tend to get obsessed about one issue—enrolment numbers. Does your strategic plan include increased enrolments as a priority area? For some owners it is the only priority. Your hope might be that the strategic plan will improve student outcomes which will lead to an enhanced reputation and then increased enrolments. Your owner or Board might not share your long-term timeline. They might direct your attention away from pedagogy and back to the bottom-line. You might find yourself at school fairs in shopping malls or debating the merits of referral bonuses when what you really want to be doing is 'The Plan'.

To meet some of these challenges your plan, and your presentation of it, will rely on evidence.

> REFLECTION
> **On traction:** Can we keep traction under our plans?
> **On the owners/board:** How should we respond when the owners/board have other priorities?
> **On the buy in:** Is it legitimate to provide classroom release to get teachers started on implementation?

Sources of Evidence

You might feel that your plan is compelling, rational and obvious. Others might find it less convincing. This is where evidence comes in.

Evidence can both point to and clarify problem areas for schools; the evidence itself having no emotion. It is to be hoped that the presentation of appropriate, objective evidence will cut through any subjective reaction to change. That, through evidence, consensus can be achieved.

Remember though that juries in criminal trials are asked to consider evidence but often cannot reach agreement. Their interpretations of the facts direct their judgements. Regardless of the strength of the evidence, your carefully crafted plan will be interpreted and implemented through the judgements of others. Yet, it remains that one of the most effective ways to convince people of the need for a particular change is to provide compelling evidence.

External Assessments

A natural starting point for evidence is assessment data. Most obviously external assessment data. The challenge for Principals though is the various pressures on how this evidence should be used. Everyone has an opinion. Governments and newspaper columnists believe, for example, that the publication of poor results will foster a shared sense of accountability and galvanise staffrooms into action.

Teachers and departments that are below expected benchmarks need support not condemnation. For you, the leader, this will require sophisticated management of staff morale. At what point will galvanising a staff to the moral purpose of raising results on standardised testing become professional blackmail of teachers who are already working in difficult conditions? Condemnation is one response. Trust, hope, and care might be a better response.

Yet, the evidence from external assessments cannot be ignored, especially if it is publicly available. At the same time, school leaders need to be careful that the data generated by external testing isn't the only evidence they are looking at.

As we are about to discover, annual community surveys, disciplinary records, and performance management results can also provide useful evidence on which to base plans.

Annual Surveys

Surveys can provide compelling evidence of how schools are faring in the eyes of teachers, parents, and students. If they are conducted annually over several years, they provide longitudinal evidence of a school's performance. The survey areas could include:

- Student Standards
- Student Behaviour
- School Culture
- Teachers' Practice
- Parent/Community

People in positions of leadership need this kind of evidence to determine what is working well and what is of concern.

The surveys provide a clear indication of the views of the key stakeholders regarding a range of issues including:

- Decision making
- The approachability of the leadership
- The attitude of the administration staff when dealing with parents
- The parents' confidence in the teachers
- The students' sense of safety.

The evidence revealed by the surveys can indicate areas of success and areas for improvement. This can create specific priority areas within a strategic plan.

I have used these kinds of surveys for over ten years in three very different schools and consider them essential. I am always surprised to hear that a school does not utilise them. One Principal I know claimed "We know what they're thinking". In fact, schools only know some of what some of 'they' are thinking. Leaders and teachers are often surprised and heartened by the results. Even if we think we know what "they are thinking" it cannot harm to get confirmation. We might be able to pat ourselves on the back and, at the same time, acknowledge that there is work to be done.

Performance Management

Teachers' performance management records can provide important data that indicates the strengths and weaknesses—not just of individuals—but of the staff. Lesson observations might, for example, reveal that the staff are strong in one aspect of classroom management but less in another area. Leadership can address this through professional development, planned strategically. This is covered in more detail in Chapter 6.

Discipline Referrals

Another important source of evidence is provided by schools' discipline records. The number of demerits (if used) or internal suspensions can indicate the success of the pastoral care program. Also, an analysis of the reasons for disciplinary action will indicate if there is a commonality to the concerns. The analysis can extend to an examination of the teachers making the referrals. The problem might well lie with the individual teacher rather than the students.

Pastoral Care Programs

Most schools run pastoral care programs based around a set of values. The data from student behaviour records can inform us if the program has been successful or not. It might cause a review of the strategy or the adoption of a different approach. Awards programs that are intended to recognise students' achievements can be reviewed to provide data on the types of success being seen and those not occurring.

Incident Records

Schools should be maintaining a register of incidents. These records can provide valuable data relating to safety and response to issues around safety.

> **REFLECTION**
>
> **On evidence**: Is it true that there are no facts, only interpretations?
> **On the use of Evidence:** What evidence is your school currently collecting? How is it being used?

Responsibility for the Priority Areas

The responsibility for developing and implementing a priority area should not be exclusively the responsibility of the Principal. Most schools will have a leadership team. This team is an important asset if the strategic plan has several priority areas. It can provide deputy Principals and stage leaders with an opportunity to experience school wide leadership. It will be the leader's responsibility to nominate who will lead the Priority Area, its progress and accountability. An exercise in trust.

Priority Areas can also provide an opportunity for capacity building with teachers (Chapter 7). A problem I experienced was that many teachers are not interested in leadership. The reason for their hesitancy included the time required, the perception of their peers, and a lack of confidence in their ability to lead. One solution was to form a committee of teachers to manage each priority area. This approach assuaged the concerns of the individual teacher. The workload is shared, there is no single spotlight, and the group created its own confidence. 'Management' of the area became 'leadership' of it, organically.

However, a word of caution. While we want staff to have a sense of ownership of their Priority Area and the larger plan itself, that does not absolve leaders (i.e. you) of responsibility for the overall success of the plan. You will need to keep track of the progress and potholes encountered. Regular meetings with the committees to provide you with updates are essential.

My Strategic Plans

In any school there are many issues and concerns competing for attention. We cannot solve them all with one strategic plan. We must be selective. The evidence must guide our decision making. Which evidence is the most compelling? Which evidence makes you think "we have a problem here".

My first Strategic Plan was over ambitious. It was a serious case of overreach. It could be described as a scattergun approach. If I fired enough shots, I'd hit something. The plan did not achieve the changes I had hoped for, but it was a learning exercise. It taught me to be strategic.

My second Strategic Plan had fewer priority areas and more compelling evidence. One priority area within it won a State award for excellence and was part of a national research project into effective mathematics teaching. The fourth plan won a national award for significantly improving students' writing results on external testing. At the core of this plan was a reimagining of professional development (Chapter 7).

Strategic plans try to create a different future. They try to provide focus and purpose. They must be based on evidence. They need to allow for collaboration during their inception and their implementation. They might need adjustments as the implementation unfolds.

My Educated Life

> *Coffs Harbour, Australia*
>
> After a decade in Coffs, the successful strategic plans outlined above contributed significantly to an improvement in the parents' perception of the school. This in turn helped lift enrolments. It improved student outcomes. It brought the staff together in a shared mission. It also contributed to staff stability. Success can be a glue that binds us.
>
> We achieved a lot. Life was good. Yet, as time passed, I realised I needed a change.
>
> As a reflexive leader you know when your effectiveness has reduced, and your interest has dwindled. It is necessary, but sometimes uncomfortable, to face the truth that you need a reboot.
>
> My next appointment was certainly different from picturesque Coffs Harbour. It was to a place that is sometimes referred to as the 'heart of darkness.'

In this chapter we have looked at the role of strategic planning in achieving a reimagination of schools. Strategic plans provide a road map to address the concerns raised by the evidence; maps which provide the route, but rarely predict the bumps in the road.

In the next chapter we'll look at how 'leading the learning' might ease the journey.

LEADING THE REIMAGINING

"The real role of leadership in education is not command and control. The real role of leadership is climate control, creating a climate of possibility"

Ken Robinson

In the previous chapter we looked at reimagining schools through a specific plan. A process which requires 'talking the talk'. In this chapter I present the second of the strategies a Principal can adopt to lead change: 'leading learning', or 'instructional leadership'. In other words, as a leader you must *'walk the walk'* of the reimagining. You must *model* the change.

My Educated Life

Port Moresby, Papua New Guinea, 2009-14
It is said that there are three types of foreigners who accept employment in Papua New Guinea (PNG): mercenaries, madmen, and missionaries. In my six years in PNG, I suspect I met the criteria for all three types.

I was the mercenary who accepted an employment contract that significantly increased my annual salary. I was also comfortable with the business class annual flights home. The large colonial house and domestic help were very welcome. As was the brand-new *Kia Sportage*. Yes, it was an extraordinary employment contract. But there was a price to pay. PNG has a reputation for violence and disorder. Daily life had many restrictions. Nightlife was downright dangerous.

I was the madman who proposed to the Board of Governors that we should reduce the school enrolment by 120 students. The lunatic who convinced the Board that the financial hit was in the best interests of the school.

I was also like a missionary, bringing Western education to an impoverished nation. I would proselytise about differentiation with my staff and seek 'conversions' to strategic planning amongst the Assistant Principals I was sent to mentor.

My new school, *Korobosea International*, is a well-established school in the capital city, Port Moresby. A city that is regularly on the list of the ten most dangerous in the world. It was the school of choice for the Prime Minister's children. My arrival coincided with the beginning of the biggest foreign project in PNG's history. Exxon Mobil began pumping liquid natural gas from massive reserves in the highlands. The economic circumstances of the city were changing. Wealthy foreigners arrived, lucrative positions for nationals were created, and local businesses suddenly had cashed-up customers. The boom benefitted us all.

Reimagining Through Leadership

School improvement–reimagining our schools–requires effective and reflexive leadership. We might have a good plan, but it will be a learning journey. A journey that will need leaders who are willing to learn and collaborate, not simply direct and command. Successful reimagining will require '*buy in*' by the leaders, not just the staff.

Viviane Robinson in her meta-study of Principal effectiveness identified five dimensions of leadership that contribute to the improvement of schools. The highest rated element was leadership that was 'promoting and participating in teacher learning and development. Note the use of '*participating in*'[1].

Building on Robinson's work, Judith Chapman's report for the OECD examined the presence of 'promotion and participation in teacher learning' in the school development plans of seventeen countries. Most included an expectation that school Principals would be leading the learning of their staff[2].

Similarly, in his highly influential 'Visible Learning', John Hattie lists 252 influences on student learning, from most effective to least. Hattie notes that the 'number one factor that impacts student learning is engaging teaching.' As a result, he believes schools must look at:

---

1. Robinson V (2007) 'School Leadership and Student Outcomes', ACEL Monograph Series No 41, October, p21

2. Chapman J (2008) 'Learning Centric Leadership', OECD Report, Paris, January p9

> "...changing the culture of education so that teachers are excited about teaching, and students are excited and engaged in learning".[3]

Or, simply put, all of the studies point to the importance of leading through teaching.

Instructional Leadership: Leading Teachers & Leading Through Teaching

School leaders must be exemplary at modelling the behaviours and practices they value. What a Principal does, and what they are seen to do, is repeated and amplified throughout their school.

Taking a teaching role is one way in which Principals can *'walk that walk'*.

There are many advantages to Principals maintaining a teaching role. It retains their appreciation of the demanding work of their staff. It might contribute to the de-privatising of classroom practice. It is an opportunity to build trust and allay the apprehension of teachers who feel vulnerable around 'the Boss.' Principals might enjoy working with students.

Making a commitment to maintain a teaching load, when your job description no longer specifies it, might seem simple enough but the demands and complexity of leading large schools can conspire to undermine this good intention. One solution might be taking a support teaching role where your sudden absence is not critical. It could also suggest a level of humbleness—not a bad attribute for leaders.

---

3. Larmer J (ND) 'Boosting Student Engagement', Educators Blog Defined

If for some of the time you are 'in the trenches' with your teachers, you're likely to enhance your credibility. You'll give teachers hope. You'll have shown how deeply you care. You might also gain valuable insights into where the plans are working and where they aren't. You'll better empathise with what staff feel about the plans and why.

Leading as a Source of Advice

Another example of Principals leading learning is to be a source of advice.

Imagine being approached by a teacher for advice in developing a spelling program or the teaching of a mathematics unit. Such an approach assumes two things. The first is that the teacher has sufficient trust in you to reveal their lack of knowledge. The second is that you will have some answers. This will require currency in the craft of teaching, not administrative or financial expertise. As any reimagining unfolds there will be staff in need of support and advice—will you be the one to provide it? Will you be leading the learning?

Robinson cites research that indicates that Principals in high achieving schools have:

> "...a higher level of knowledge about instructional matters than their colleagues in low achieving schools."[4]

---

4. Op cit, Robinson, p16

There is an assumption that such knowledge is being made accessible to teachers via Principals' pedagogic expertise.

Teachers involved in a significant reimagining of pedagogy will need support. Things rarely go right the first time. Most people enter an 'implementation dip' as they reimagine their teaching, the curriculum, school structures ... whatever the plan identified as a priority area. They may feel inadequate, perhaps even incompetent. This is when you need to provide those three resources—trust, hope, and care but also, on occasions, specific pedagogical advice. Such guidance, coming from someone who has been in the trenches, is likely to be better received.

Leading Professional Development

It is my belief that Principals should be closely involved in the design and delivery of their school's professional learning.

In Belgium, Holland, and New Zealand it is government policy that teachers' professional development (PD) be based within schools and be developed and led by the Principal. However, we should be mindful of Reeves' warning that:

> "In many school systems, professional development continues to rely on a combination of inspirational speeches by outside experts followed by stern warnings from administrators."[5]

---

5. Op cit, Chapman, p29

Another challenge for leaders developing PD is highlighted by Judy Smeed who notes a trend towards schools contracting their professional development to 'outside agencies.' Smeed believes this is a result of school leaders being unable to lift their heads above the day-to-day melee of administrating schools.

If Principals are to lead professional development, they need to become skilled in the facilitation of teacher learning. Leading a school's PD offering requires a strong understanding of how adults learn, and the ability to create the conditions for this learning to occur. Teachers' professional learning should be modelled on the approaches we expect them to use in their work with children. All too often it isn't. Reeves observes:

> "Is there not a hint of irony in cramming five hundred teachers into an auditorium to hear someone talk about the need for 'differentiated' instruction."[6]

One way to conceptualise teachers' professional learning is as a two-phase process.

The first phase involves exposure to the change. This could occur through observing colleagues, presentations with an external expert, through personal research, or with a mentor.

The second phase provides opportunities to trial, refine, and critique the change.

---

6. Reeves D (2008) 'Leadership and Learning', ACEL Monograph Series, No 43, September, p11

The second phase is the key to successful professional development, but all too often there is no provision for this phase. Without the second phase the exposure from the first phase is unlikely to achieve any traction. Leading learning is about ensuring that teachers get this opportunity. It will cost, and usually more than the exposure phase. Yet, without it the money expended on the initial phase will most likely result in no improvement.

Leading the Learning of Leaders

Much has been written about an emerging vacuum in school leadership. This suggests that an important aspect of contemporary school leadership is developing the next generation of school leaders.

School leadership is essentially about exercising judgement. That's really what we get paid for. We make judgement calls every day about students, staff, resourcing, financing, even about the parking lot. For most Principals our judgement is based on years of experience. This book is about sharing some of mine with you.

My Educated Life

Port Moresby, Papua New Guinea

My six years in Papua New Guinea were some of the most professionally rewarding of my career.

In addition to my role as a Principal I was involved in a mentoring program for young national Principals. I also led reviews of other schools. This provided me with an opportunity to see PNG from the outer islands

> to the remote highlands. It's a place of extremes, in both geography and culture. There are over 800 different languages spoken. I developed a deep and enduring affection for this wild and challenging land. On many occasions I have imagined returning to its dusty and unpredictable roads. We will revisit it in later chapters.
>
> PNG was where I learned the importance of walking the leader's walk.

Leading by example is another aspect of effectively leading a reimagining.

This can occur in different ways. It might be through designing a professional development program, taking a teaching role, or being a source of advice for classroom practice. In essence, following all the talking which resulted in the Strategic Plan, it's *'walking the walk'*. It's doing and getting things done. It's personally delivering on the promises of the plan. Some days you'll do a lot of talking, but, as a leader, it's critical that you also get out there–that you lead the reimagining from the front.

In the next chapter we will look at a specific process for leading and supporting teachers in their own act of imagination.

PERFORMANCE MANAGEMENT AN ACT OF (RE)IMAGINATION

"Management is efficiency in climbing the ladder of success; leadership determines whether the ladder is leaning against the right wall." **Stephen R. Covey**

Reimagining a school requires constant communication. It requires clear intentions and expectations. It may require asking teachers to change their pedagogy—which they might well regard as adequate, perhaps even excellent. It will require specifying exactly what is expected. It will require providing support for people to meet those expectations and managing their performance.

If Chapter 4 was about *'talking the talk'* and Chapter 5 about you, the leader, *'walking the walk'*, then this chapter is about taking other people on the journey with you—helping them to *'walk a new walk'*.

My Educated Life

Johor Bahru, Malaysia, 2015-16

Changi International Airport in Singapore is considered one of the world's best. My flight from Sydney arrived in the early afternoon of December 31st, 2014. Another part of my 'educated life' was about to begin.

> As soon as I emerged from immigration an elderly Malaysian woman approached me. Her name was Puan Sarah. She wore a traditional black hijab conspicuously matched with a bright red jacket similar to that worn by Michael Jackson in the *Thriller* video. It was the first of many juxtapositions that my new appointment would provide. Outside, a convoy of black vehicles pulled up. A man exited the lead vehicle, a *Mercedes Benz*. He opened the door of the second vehicle, an immaculate *Toyota Sienna*. Inside, two large armchairs dominated the space. In one sat an elderly Malay woman, known to all as 'Madam D'. The convoy carried her entourage. The first vehicle carried her two brothers. I joined her in the second. The third vehicle contained her secretary and niece. The fourth carried her personal chef and maid.
>
> Mdm D owned and operated private schools across Malaysia. She was first and foremost a businesswoman, having made her fortune constructing toll roads in the booming Malaysian economy of the 1980s. She had properties around the world and owned at least thirty cars. A mother of five children she was gregarious and parsimonious in equal measures. As I was about to discover, she expected her schools to turn a profit.

PERFORMANCE MANAGEMENT

An Australian *Minister for School Education*, Peter Garret, once declared that teachers were 'entitled' to performance management. His use of the word 'entitled' surprised people. Teachers' contracts entitle them to wages, holidays, and sick leave, but performance management was an unexpected inclusion. Given that 63% of teachers believe that performance evaluation is only to fulfil official requirements, it was probably also unwelcome.[1]

The figure of 63% seems conservative. Few teachers like or enjoy having their performance managed. Some fear the consequences. Others are cynical of its intentions. Few see it as supportive.

Your challenge as a leader is to resolve this contradiction. To help you, my hope in this chapter is to rehabilitate this vital aspect of school management.

Let's start that process with a few questions:

- Where the law allows, should performance management be tied to contract renewal and continued employment?

- Should performance management be used only with teachers in their first years of service—a form of probation?

- Or, should all teachers be under some form of performance management?

- If not, how do we manage the performance of long serving staff? Do we need to?

- Can we risk alienating teachers through performance management at a time when recruitment and retention are increasingly difficult?

---

1. 'Australian Teacher Performance and Development Framework', AITSL, August 2012, p1

Whatever your own answers and whatever your own sense of its value, we know from the evidence that, done well, performance management:

- Can change schools for the better.

- Helps in providing clear pedagogical expectations.

- Improves teachers' performance—in turn improving student outcomes.

- Can strike a balance between support and productive pressure.

- Provides a clear paper trail in cases where employment is terminated for underperformance.

What follows are three examples when performance management contributed to educational reimaginings. The examples come from different schools, in different countries, and with different purposes. They are framed around the (hopefully) by now familiar precepts of **trust**, **hope**, and **care**.

In the first example, from Papua New Guinea, the role of performance management in staff selection is highlighted. We need to appoint the right teachers and we need to support them. We need to support their **hopes** and aspirations as professionals. In the second example, from Malaysia, performance management is at the centre of a shift from 'traditional' teaching to contemporary pedagogy. Involving the whole staff, many of whom were reluctant, it required large doses of **care**. The final example, from Australia, is an example of teachers adopting a new technology. Once again it was performance management which provided the framework for the transition. It was an investment in **trust**.

> **REFLECTION**
> **On Performance Management**: What causes some teachers to resist performance management?

Performance Management and Probation

So much of leadership is the exercise of judgement.

Of the many judgements you will make, recruitment is the single most important. It is a judgement call that will affect your school's quality and culture...and your own professional reputation. For better or for worse, you will have to live with these decisions.

Which is where, the law and context allowing, probation comes in.

During my time with the *International Education Agency* (IEA) of Papua New Guinea I was involved in a very thorough probation system. The process culminated in 'Moderation'. Moderation required teachers to provide a work portfolio justifying their selection for permanent employment. Failure meant termination. It meant a loss of job, income, support, and social status. The stakes were high.

The stakes were also high for the schools. If successful at Moderation, teachers would be offered five-year contracts. Five years is a long time to have an underperforming teacher on your staff.

For many teachers, success required an act of reimagination. It required a perceptual and practical shift from the education they had received (as children themselves) to the education they were now expected to provide (as teachers). This wasn't easy. Most had been educated in schools with

45 students to a class. Rote learning was the primary means of instruction. There were few resources and corporal punishment stood in for pastoral care.

As the next example shows, my story of Kopi Wapi, the act of imagination that these teachers were required to make was substantial.

> **My Kopi Wapi Story**
>
> The critical point in Moderation was the Principal's final recommendation – a stark tick, '*Yes*' or '*No*'. For most teachers it was a straightforward affirmation, an easy '*Yes*'. However, there are occasions when Principals face a difficult choice. In 2013, I faced one such choice. I had to decide the fate of three teachers. Sarah and Sharon were straightforward. They had displayed all the professional standards expected. '*Yes*'. The third, Kopi, was not so simple.
>
> The evidence from Kopi's Moderation was not good. He had numerous absences, missed deadlines, and his classroom performance was erratic. Yet, he was also one of the nicest men you could meet. He was gentle, humble, and had a genuine interest in teaching.
>
> Kopi's assessment was on my desk, waiting for the tick or cross, when my PA informed me that he was outside, requesting a meeting. I hesitated given the proximity of my decision but decided to see him. Kopi began by explaining how important his employment was. One of his daughters was unwell and in need of regular medical attention. The rent on their house had recently been

increased. His elderly parents back in the village relied on his income for their survival. Kopi became emotional as he explained his situation. He began to cry. My PA joined the meeting, consoled him, but then led Kopi out.

I faced a dilemma. The safety and wellbeing of a teacher (and his family) set against potentially years of poor teaching affecting hundreds of children (and their fee-paying parents). It was also important to honour the performance management system and the hard work of the successful teachers.

I ticked the '*No*' box. Kopi left the school at the end of the year. He accepted the decision and there was no animosity. However, I feared for his future.

Several months later I was having dinner in one of Port Moresby's best restaurants. I looked across the room and saw a familiar face sitting at a table of *Exxon* executives. It was Kopi. He'd secured a position with *Exxon* as a community relations officer. He had a better salary and a better house. His daughter was well and his life much improved. He was much happier.

The right call for the school turned out to be the right call for him. Yet, it could have gone the other way. It would have been easier to tick '*Yes*'.

There are times when leaders are required to make difficult decisions. This was one such time. I knew that ticking '*Yes*' would have legitimised poor teaching. I would have been protecting a person's employment, not stewarding pedagogy. Culling might be crude (and hard), but sometimes it is necessary.

The point of the Kopi Wapa story? That having a robust performance management system in place helped. To some extent, it depersonalised the decision. It certainly professionalised it. Kopi could see where he was underperforming. It was documented. Evidenced. Perhaps this is why he accepted the decision with grace.

> **REFLECTION**
> **On Probation**:
> Have you lived to regret an appointment? What did you do to address the regret?
> Have you lived to see an appointment blossom? How was this achieved?
> Should performance management only be used with teachers in the early years of their career?
> How robust is the 'paper trail' in your current school where a teacher is underperforming?

Performance Management–A Guided Reimagination

The example above, Kopi's story, illustrates the value of performance management for individual staff. The second example takes a whole-school perspective—a major act of collective reimagining.

I was once told that: "*Teachers teach the way they were taught.*"

I have seen the truth of this in classrooms in Papua New Guinea, Australia, Indonesia, Vietnam, and Malaysia. Too many teachers deliver monologues. They stand at the front and talk. They pronounce. They proclaim. Maybe occasionally they ask a question or two. But they are the 'sage on the stage.'

This approach presumes legitimacy through old and trusted methodologies. It is how many teachers were taught and is the method through which they teach.

It needs to change. It certainly needed to change at a school I led in Malaysia.

We were transitioning from a 'local' private academy, offering a limited academic programme, to an international school, offering a full international curriculum and appropriate pedagogy. Like the teachers in Papua New Guinea, most of the staff's own experience of schooling had been rote and punitive. They would be asked to adopt teaching methods they had never experienced themselves.

The *Council of International Schools* accreditation expects that:

> "...the performance management system is defined and implemented for all faculty based on pre-determined, explicit criteria, and is *supported by a program of professional development which is linked to appraisal outcomes.*" [my emphasis][2].

This linkage of professional development and appraisal outcomes was key to the transition of this school. Performance management and professional development worked in tandem to transition from 'chalk and talk' to contemporary pedagogy.

---

2. Machin D (2019) 'The Organisational Evolution of Contemporary International Schools', Journal of Research in International Education, P116

One of the most successful strategies was to ask the staff to list the elements they would expect to observe in a great lesson. This was the beginning of the reimagining. We reviewed videos of 'great teaching' and recounted tales of our own 'best teachers', identifying and discussing what made them great. This process produced a set of collectively agreed appraisal outcomes that was an amalgamation of the staff's expectations of a quality lesson. It was sufficiently collaborative for the staff to feel that they had had a role in creating the standards by which they would be judged. It demonstrated a level of trust in their capability.

Based on the observations which followed, I began providing professional development which covered the areas needing attention. This was the support teachers needed. I then observed lessons with an expectation of seeing the new practice in action. This was the pressure teachers needed. It was professional development and performance management working in tandem.

Equally, it was important to emphasise to the staff that this was a developmental process. We weren't expecting them to achieve all the outcomes in the first observation. This settled most of the disquiet. I suggested it would be a two-year project. In fact, within a year most teachers had transformed their lessons. The act of imagination had become reality. There was plenty of anecdotal and empirical evidence that:

- Students' behaviour improved significantly.

- Students were more engaged.

- Teachers' job satisfaction increased.

- Parents' confidence in the teachers increased.

The lesson I learnt, and one I hope the above conveys, is that professional learning and performance management are two sides of the same coin. Together they provide the framework for change.

> ### My Gorilla Story
>
> Few people enjoy it. Some resent it. Others distrust it. Some need it, but avoid it.
>
> Lesson observations. The weird, scary, vulnerable but very necessary experience of having another adult (perhaps other adults) in your classroom, watching you do your job.
>
> I have a presentation I use to convince teachers of the importance of observation. One of the key arguments I provide is the *'Invisible Gorilla Experiment.'* In the experiment people watch a video of players passing a basketball and are asked to count the number of passes. At one point a person in a gorilla suit walks amongst the basketballers, beats their chest, and walks off. Most people don't see the gorilla, they are too focused on counting the passes. This is called selective attention.
>
> As the observers we see the gorillas that the teachers do not. The teacher's attention is elsewhere, on the multiple aspects of lesson delivery. We can look for the gorillas. We can provide feedback on the things teachers don't see.

Performance Management–Technology

Our final example illustrates how performance management can guide and support the implementation of new technology.

Technology has challenges unlike any other reimagining. There is a technical component to it that, for some, is threatening. Others might see little need to change, no matter how good the technology. Others would rather funds had been spent elsewhere. Technology stirs emotions other changes might not.

In 2002 the priority for my school in Australia was a transition from blackboards to interactive whiteboards (IWB) and a new set of associated pedagogies. A reimagining that would push the school into the twenty-first century.

Training and development included a performance management process to provide support and pressure. A list of competencies was created to guide and evaluate the adoption. It was relatively easy to break the technical side down—turn on, turn off. However, there was still reluctance from some of the older staff. Their competence and resilience would be on public display.

As the implementation unfolded it provided a valuable lesson. I anticipated that the older teachers would find the adoption difficult. Some of the older staff opposed even considering the IWBs. This affected other staff. I decided to ask one of the naysayers to be a pioneer—one of the first to have an IWB installed in her room and to undertake the training. Keep your friends close and your enemies closer?

Lucy was a self-described 'crusty old dinosaur' with Luddite tendencies. She was hesitant, it would expose her lack of knowledge about IT generally. She would need to rely on others for assistance. She would be vulnerable. However, she accepted and joined the early adopter's group. It was very challenging for her, but she eventually achieved a high level of competence. One of her proudest achievements was the screensaver she installed on her IWB—the image of a traditional blackboard! The responsibility of leading the implementation created an advocate out of an opponent. An enthusiast out of a denier.

> **REFLECTION**
> **On Technology?** Does introducing new technology have additional challenges for older staff)

IS PERFORMANCE MANAGEMENT NECESSARY?

Lucy's story raises a final question: *"Do experienced teachers need performance management?"*

Many teachers would argue they don't. They can be trusted to be prepared, to provide stimulating lessons, and to maintain student engagement. They are deserving of management's trust.

At the beginning of this chapter I noted that 63% of teachers believe that performance management is only done to fulfil administration requirements. I would guess that older teachers made up the majority of this 63%. It is the group most likely to resist lesson observations, program evaluations, assessment checks, and new technology. To maintain the currency and enthusiasm of this cohort is a challenge, but there are solutions:

- Create a culture of continual improvement.
- Ask these teachers to arrange peer partnerships for their observations.
- Ask them to lead the performance management of younger staff. As mentors, they might also learn something.
- Ask them to lead new ideas or approaches, to be the pioneers.

We need to show respect for these teachers but, at the same time, challenge any stasis.

My Educated Life

> *Johor Bahru, Malaysia*
>
> Johor Bahru was a brief sojourn. Within six months the owner asked me to move to Kuala Lumpur and manage her flagship school. The parents of the Johor Bahru school complained that I should at least finish the year with their school. The compromise was that I would manage two schools 350 kms apart. Two days a week in Johor Bahru and three days a week in Kuala Lumpur.
>
> Initially, it was a solution I was happy with. I was provided with a good car and two apartments. The highway between the two cities is excellent.
>
> Yet, the experience soon began to sour.
>
> The commute became tedious and, moreover, so were the increasing demands of 'for profit' schools.

> It became clear that trust, hope, and care were in limited supply. There was little sense of purpose – other than cost saving. I became disillusioned with schools.
>
> My next placement would bring a regeneration of belief in the power of education.

If we want to improve the quality of teaching in our schools, performance management is a necessity. I agree with Peter Garret that it is an entitlement. We need a performance management process which both provides support and applies productive pressure.

Teachers should regard performance management as a right not a threat.

TEACHERS

"If we are truly effective teachers, then we are creating autonomous, independent, and self-directed learners."

Robert John Meehan

Not all reimaginings are great and grand designs.

Dedicated teachers are constantly reimagining. They might not be plotting educational revolutions, but they do plan evolutions. How will they differentiate? How might they tweak their lessons? Should they change their reward system?

These simple changes are valuable forms of reimagining. They are also indicators of a strong school culture.

In this chapter we will look at ways of providing the conditions for teachers to reimagine, and to evolve their pedagogy. I will present two strategies: **self-direction** and **capacity building**. Each contributed to creating successful workplaces in my previous schools. Each improved recruitment and retention. We begin in a small town in southern Malaysia.

My Educated Life

Muar, Malaysia, 2017-22

Muar is a small, provincial town in the southern Malaysian state of Johor. Located on the Straits of Malacca it is a quiet backwater of traditional Malaysia.

From 2017 to 2019 I shuttled between Muar, my home in Sydney, and my partner's home in Saigon. I had been appointed to be the Principal of *Destiny Academy* which was in the process of transforming into *Destiny International*. Land had been purchased and plans drawn up for a purpose-built school. Bureaucracy delayed progress, and it was decided that I should take a role as a consultant until the building and licensing were completed. Thus, I flew in for one week each month to lead the transition in readiness for the day *Destiny International* opened.

Eventually, with a new building, and a government licence, *Destiny International* was opened as a *Cambridge Exam Centre*. The licensing with State and National authorities had been completed. It had been a long and arduous process for the Board and senior staff. A process made longer and more arduous by the Board's implacable determination not to 'ease' the process. No brown paper envelopes, no winks, and no nods. It added years to the process, but the management had modelled the integrity it expected of its staff and students.

As the above suggests, the management at *Destiny* is progressive. The parents are supportive, the students well behaved.

> Yet, as in so many schools, teacher recruitment and retention are an issue. For Destiny, the problem lies in the school's geography; for urbanised teacher training graduates it is simply too remote, the nearest major city too far away.
>
> For me, and hopefully for you, the reader, *Destiny* is a lesson that, despite your best efforts, and despite a supportive culture and strong collegiality, sometimes there are factors beyond your control.

The Situation

Any attempt to reimagine or improve education will start and end with teachers.

The professional situation for most teachers has been deteriorating for decades. They have been devalued by communities and by governments. Their workloads have become unreasonable. The purchasing power of their salaries has declined. There is an increasing ambivalence towards the value of education. Many teachers are asking themselves:

"Do I really want to keep doing this?"

This raises two questions. The first is: How to address teacher retention rates that are withering faster than replacement rates? And the second: In the face of disrespect, poor pay, and threats to their wellbeing, why would anyone aspire to become a teacher?

> **REFLECTION**
> **On the Situation:** Why did you become a teacher? Do those reasons remain true today?
> Do they remain true for new teachers entering the profession?
> In your context, are teachers leaving? Why?

Recruitment and Retention

Recent surveys from Finland and Sweden revealed that one third of teachers under the age of 24 had left the profession. On the other side of the world, the Vietnamese Education Ministry recently forecast that it will face a shortage of 55,000 pre-school teachers by 2030. The Ministry disclosed that:

> "...the toughest challenge in the recruitment of teachers is the fact that they are quitting in droves over work pressure, long hours, and low income."[1]

There are schools where recruitment and retention are not an issue. These schools are attractive to people who aspire to be great teachers. They are schools with good reputations for collaboration, and communication. I have been privileged to contribute to schools with this kind of culture. There are two specific strategies that I developed in these schools that positively affected the recruitment/retention problem. They are strategies worthy of your consideration.

The first is to recognise that high performance teachers expect a level of self-direction. The second, is that capacity building helps to create a supportive but ambitious culture.

---

1. Binh Minh 'Vietnam Will Lack 55 400 Teachers', VN Express, 5/04/24

Combined they can create a great place to spend your working life.

By providing opportunities for self-direction and capacity building we can have a positive effect on retention. Teachers who have a sense of control over their professional lives are more likely to have job satisfaction. They are more likely to stay in jobs they enjoy. And, when you do need to recruit, you can expect a substantial number of applicants – all looking to join an organisation built on trust, care and hope.

> **REFLECTION**
> **On Recruitment and Retention:** Are recruitment and retention an issue in your context? If so, what are the causes? Are they within your control to mitigate?
>
> Is there a strong sense of community amongst the teachers you work with? How can leadership develop a strong community?

The Self-Directed Teacher

If we want to retain our teachers, we need to give them reasons to stay. We need to give them ownership, a safe and attractive environment, control over the curriculum (as far as possible), and some control of their professional development.

Yet, how much autonomy do we actually provide?

Most classroom teachers would agree that their job is made easier and more rewarding when students take charge of their learning. The same can be said of teachers. Yet, too often the curriculum requires high levels of fidelity with little or no independence (for learners or teachers).

Too often professional development is tied to government initiatives, departmental priorities, or school plans and not to individual needs. Too often teachers' experience of professional development is *'one size fits all.'*

Seymour Sarason was one of the most influential educators of the twentieth century. Michael Fullan and Andy Hargreaves co-wrote his obituary. Sarason was a strong advocate for self-directed learning. He wrote:

> "For our schools to do better than they do we have to give up the belief that it is possible to create the conditions for productive learning when those conditions do not exist for educational personnel."[2]

If we want to retain capable teachers, we need to create the conditions for job satisfaction. Self-direction is a strategy that can contribute significantly to these conditions.

In 2004 I faced these challenges at my school in Coffs Harbour. I asked myself: *"What would teachers' professional learning look like if it were self-directed?"*

The answer to my question was:

- Immersion with the curriculum and independent development of curriculum replacement units.
- Examining, benchmarking and discussing students' work (with students and colleagues).

---

2. Ringuet Tanya 'Transforming Teachers' Australian Educational Leader, Vol 34 No 1 2012, ACEL

- Study groups and case discussions.
- Coaching and mentoring.
- Forming partnerships with other schools and with parents, and developing partnerships with non-teaching professionals.
- Attending workshops and completing university courses.

I decided to provide teachers with the opportunity to self-direct their Professional Development, but I also wanted the PD to be tied to a Priority Area within our Strategic Plan (Chapter 4). Evidence from national testing indicated that our results in Writing were below the results achieved in Reading and Mathematics. I offered teachers the opportunity to self-direct their professional learning. The only requirement was that it had to have improving Writing as the focus.

Time is the key. I bought the teachers time to work on their chosen projects. I did this by saving money from the annual budget—we reduced spending on textbooks and technology. The money saved was used to provide teachers with time. Substitute teachers were employed to cover the teachers on the days they pursued their own learning. Time gave the teachers an opportunity to exercise autonomy.

This professional learning program achieved a great deal and was recognised with National and State awards. We were given substantial prize money and an all-expenses paid trip to meet the Minister for Education. More importantly, we achieved significant and sustained improvements in the students' Writing results. Our achievements included:

- The creation of a K-6 Writing continuum.
- A webpage, survey and training to support parents.
- Understanding our students' knowledge of Writing through a 'learning as informant approach.'
- A new Writing 'Scope and Sequence', with resources to support it.
- A cross-sectoral support group for kindergarten teachers.
- A shared editing symbols system.
- Trialling new Writing strategies.

Each of these achievements was initiated and developed by the teachers – autonomously. They used the time provided but also substantial amounts of their own free time, such was the level of 'buy-in'.

The two years of this project are the best example I have seen of teachers forming a learning community. I saw teachers collaborating on projects, teaching each other, and 'leading the learning' during presentations. The levels of collaboration and collegiality were exemplary. There was a clarity of purpose amongst the staff.

The project was not without its challenges. Some teachers went down dead-ends, others were unable to determine what they wanted to do; some fretted over the amount of time they were spending away from their class. There were times when I had to provide large amounts of **trust**, **hope**, and **care** as teachers navigated a different approach to PD.

Over the ten years of leading this school we had only a few resignations. A teacher survey indicated a very high level of satisfaction with the PD provision. We also added headcount due to increased enrolments. The application rate for vacant positions was astounding.

There are many factors that contribute to teachers' job satisfaction. We cannot control them all, but some we can. Self-direction is a good place to start.

> **REFLECTION**
> **On Self Directed PD**: Is 'buying time' for staff a legitimate way to get 'buy in'? Is it seed money? Should *all* PD be self-directed?

Capacity Building

The second strategy I have used to address the retention and recruitment problem is capacity building. Capacity building has great potential to contribute to teachers' job satisfaction which, in turn, improves retention. Throughout 'my educated life' capacity building has contributed significantly to each school's success.

Capacity building is developing the capability of all people within a school. It is an attitude you bring to your school. It starts with an assumption that people want to do their best in their chosen occupation – and not just those already in leadership positions. You build capacity at all levels of the organisation. You are optimistic about everyone's abilities and intentions.

One of the best examples of capacity building I have was the maintenance team at my school in PNG. An all-male team, they had low levels of literacy but high levels of technical ability. As they came to understand that I trusted their judgement and skills, they reciprocated by becoming one of the most effective and reliable teams I have ever worked with. Eventually they had responsibility for the rolling maintenance of a site with over 40 classrooms, 15 staff residences, and numerous sporting facilities. They ordered materials, they prioritised the jobs, and they initiated projects to improve the campus.

How does capacity building with a maintenance team affect teacher retention? The work of the team affected the teachers in several ways. The first was seen in the annual staff surveys. The results indicated that the staff were taking pride in the school's appearance. It was an attractive place to work. The second was the maintenance team's timely responses to problems in the classrooms. Stuck windows were unstuck, door locks mended, and power sockets repaired. Finally, the teaching staff could see my sincerity in developing a team that had previously spent its time, well, wasting time, in a shed at the back of the school. My willingness to invest in this group was a sign to the whole staff that I was 'walking the walk'.

I tried the same approach with the Grade Leaders at the school. There were six teachers in each grade. It was surprising to me that there was no formal leadership of the grades. The previous Principal had strong autocratic tendencies and his trust in the staff had been restricted to a few 'favourites.' The resulting culture could be characterised as cautious and suspicious. Implementing a reimagining of leadership into this culture needed generous portions of trust, hope and care.

None of the teachers appointed as Grade Leaders had any previous experience of leadership. They would need mentoring and support. I held weekly meetings with them as a team. I encouraged them to share their concerns and successes. They came to realise I was willing to trust their judgement. This was an important contribution to their growing self-belief. They also understood that significant amounts of my time were being invested in their development. The eventual success was built on the relationships I developed with these teams: improved trust, reduced individual workloads, strong team cultures, and a sense of belonging. Young staff now had role models and could see potential for their own future leadership.

For my own 'educated life', one of the most important lessons I learnt is that individuals evolve into their roles. Initially people might be overly cautious. They might make mistakes. They might need time to develop self-belief. Their understanding of what you are trying to do and, most importantly, why you are trying to do it will also need time to evolve.

This example might seem anachronistic. Grade leaders are nothing unusual. It is not the creation of the team that I want to highlight, it is the development of the people within the team. Many schools have grade leaders, but they operate within a narrow remit. Their authority is limited. Real delegation of authority requires the development of a specific culture. Our grade leaders began to exercise judgement autonomously.

All fine and good, but capacity building can put you – the leader – in a vulnerable position. The buck will still stop with you. Therein lies the paradox. If you are thinking capacity building will reduce your own workload, you might need to adjust that expectation. You can expect a significant increase in your weekly meetings. There will be lots of meetings. For me: a grade leaders' meeting, an administration team meeting, a maintenance team meeting, a specialist teachers' team meeting, and the operations team meeting...the list went on. Each of these meetings were necessary to show my support for the developing teams. They were also an opportunity to hear frustrations and solutions. The meetings were also necessary to monitor progress and to hold teams accountable.

Over the course of the six years that I led this school there were no resignations. We retained all the young teachers. The grass was not greener. It was an environment in which capable teachers could thrive. We developed a culture in which the retention and recruitment of teachers was a strong heartbeat not a headache.

> **REFLECTION**
> **On Capacity Building**: Is capacity building essential to a successful organisation? Are there limits to capacity building? Where/how could you build further capacity in those you lead?

Valuing Ourselves

One of my favourite television shows is '*The Drum*', a daily news roundup which sought the opinion of various experts on the day's stories. Dr Ann was a regular guest. She was included for her expertise in education.

One of the episodes included an outburst by Dr Ann, at the time the Principal of one of Australia's leading schools.

Her issue?

> *"I have a doctorate. I am the CEO of a multi-million-dollar business. I have had years of study and sacrifice. I have decades of experience in managing schools and yet I am routinely ignored by politicians and bureaucrats who invite me onto their committees. Why? Because I am just a teacher. Why? Because I do a job, they think anyone can do. They wouldn't do it with architects or doctors or entrepreneurs."*

Across my career I have witnessed many examples to support Dr Ann's outburst. There is a widespread notion that anyone can teach. This devalues not only teachers but also education.

Education has existed in some form in all human societies. It is essential to a society's viability. A definition that has travelled with me through my educated life is that education is:

> "...the transmission of the knowledge, skills and values necessary for a society to reproduce itself."[3]

This definition works as well for hunter-gatherer groups as it does for post-industrial societies. If you break the transmission, then society will be in deep trouble. It suggests that teachers need to be valued more than they currently are.

---

3. Whilst I remember the quote, the source for this is lost in the mists of time. Google hasn't helped. The words are not my own. My apologies to the original author.

Here is an example of what happens when a society fully devalues its educators:

> In 1975, when the Khmer Rouge began to take Cambodia back to Year Zero, the first victims of the genocide were the nation's teachers. Cambodian society lost the people essential to its reproduction.
>
> After the Khmer Rouge were defeated, Cambodia began its reconstruction. The process was slow and fragmented. The fabric of Cambodian society had been torn apart. The needles that sew the fabric, teachers, had been eradicated. The loss of three generations of teachers was a primary factor in the slow pace of economic and cultural recovery. Without teachers societies lose their primary survival mechanism—education.

Teachers must demand respect. Not just from students and parents but also from owners, and governments. One school owner I know illustrated this lack of respect and the widespread belief that anybody could be a teacher. She had five children and appointed each one to senior positions in her schools. The youngest son was appointed Head of Curriculum. When this twenty-year-old suggested to his mother that he might not be qualified for the position she retorted:

"You went to school didn't you!"

Next time you are asked what you do for a living don't reply:

"I'm just a teacher."

It is difficult to see how we will retain and recruit teachers if this devaluing of the profession continues, especially if we are complicit in the devaluing.

My Educated Life

> *Muar, Malaysia*
>
> Muar and Destiny International provided me with a kind of redemption.
>
> After the two years of labouring in a 'for profit' school, the return to the 'not for profit' sector was liberating. It was a return to a serious implementation of a school's mission and vision, not solely the school's financial interests. My 'educated life' was valued. Strategies that I knew from experience would develop the school were welcomed. I could provide capacity building, not profit building. I could provide self-direction, not autocratic dictation.
>
> Thus, while the relative remoteness of Muar limits some of Destiny's options, particularly regarding recruitment and retention, it is a dynamic and progressive school. It is a beacon for other schools looking to make the transition to international school status.

In this chapter we have considered the situation for teachers. We have looked at the role self-direction and capacity building can play in the retention of teachers. In the next chapter we will consider those with the authority to lead the implementation of these strategies—the Principals.

PRINCIPALS

"There are no good schools without good Principals. They just don't exist".

Anne Duncan

The successful reimagining of a school will ask big questions of those with responsibility for the transition. It will ask questions of its leaders – questions of *you*.

There are various approaches to leadership, some more appropriate to a school's situation than others. Deciding which approach is '*just right*' is one of the more challenging aspects of contemporary leadership. Leadership is also full of contradictions. Ultimately though, it is the quality of leadership, of a Principal's ability to lead, that will determine success or failure.

> **My Educated Life**
>
> *Sydney, 2020-22*
>
> Sydney is a city that can sparkle. North and south of its deep water harbour, the beaches along the Pacific coast have white sand and surf. The bays are dotted with the gleaming mansions of Australia's elite. Ferries churn

crystal wakes as they steam past the glistening sails of Sydney's famous Opera House.

I was in Phnom Penh when I heard the news. It was March 11, 2020. The WHO had declared a global pandemic. My flight to Sydney later that day was cancelled. I had left my partner in Vietnam two days earlier and, following my time in Cambodia, intended to rejoin her after a short stay in Australia. How were we to know that we would be separated for 2 years and 2 weeks? Countries closed their borders. The movements of entire populations were restricted. This was Covid.

Suddenly everyone wanted to know what introverts did on their weekends. My contribution was to suggest people should read books. I recommended Gabriel Marquez's masterpiece *"Love in a Time of Cholera."* It seemed an appropriate choice for the times.

I was sharing my house in Sydney with my daughter and her husband. She is also a teacher, so I had a front row seat as schools began responding to the 'unprecedented'.

My daughter is a dedicated teacher. She was not surprised that she was expected to maintain her usual high standards. However, she *was* confused by conflicting directives about teachers' attendance. She was disappointed to be informed that she was not an 'essential worker'. She became belligerent when the Minister of Education warned teachers not to forget their responsibilities. She watched her husband, a highly paid engineer also working from home, start at 9am and finish at 5pm as her working day pushed past 8pm.

> Covid was probably even more demanding on school Principals. Somehow, they had to coordinate the most radical shift ever seen in schools. Classrooms were empty. Teachers were remote. We were all locked-down. It remains a testimony to the abilities of school leaders that the transition was achieved so quickly and so effectively.

THE SITUATION

Principals are outnumbered. There are far more teachers and even more students. Yet, it is school Principals who have responsibility for *everyone*. School leaders are not only in the minority, but they are also under very real threats. In 2024 the Australian Catholic University released the results of its annual survey of school Principals[1]. The results made headline news, for all the wrong reasons:

- 48% of Principals had been physically threatened or attacked; a 73% increase since 2011.
- 88% reported incidences of cyberbullying.
- 20% reported episodes of moderate to severe depression.
- 56% are considering early retirement.

Another international survey found that the largest percentage of school leaders' time was spent on administration. This was followed by student and staff

---

[1]. Half of Australia's School Principals Physically Attacked, The Educator, 22/4/24

welfare. Finding the time to 'lead the learning' was a major challenge[2].

No one has ever suggested that school leadership is a walk in the park, but I don't believe anyone could have predicted the extreme and relentless pressures which Principals now work under. The higher-than-normal stress levels stemming from navigating a complex global health crisis, political divisiveness, staffing shortages, and school violence are making it harder than ever for school leaders to have any sense of job satisfaction. The result? Early retirements and resignations. The recruitment and retention problem from the previous chapter is no less relevant for school leaders.

These challenges, the challenges you might face as a school leader, perhaps as a Principal, can be navigated by developing an understanding of:

- Leadership styles and their appropriateness to a school's situation.
- The inherent contradictions of leadership.
- The different roles that you might need to adopt.

It is my hope that this chapter, based on my educated life, will be of some assistance in developing these understandings.

Leadership Styles

Imagine this. I am the Head of a Primary School, and I am cleaning out a school storeroom during the Christmas holidays. The campus is empty except for me. I am the only

---

2. Gumus S, A "*Global Typology of School Principal's Time Use*" International Journal of Educational Research, Vol: 125–2024

person who can do the job. Only I can determine if an item in the storeroom should be kept or culled. Only I can arrange the shelves correctly. Only I would do this during the holidays. Of course, the reality is that anyone could probably do these tasks, but that is not what I believed at the time.

Welcome to '*leader as hero*'.

Various leadership styles have been identified, including servant-leader, autocratic, transactional, and, of course, the 'leader as hero'. The characteristics of this latter model suggest that such leaders are ambitious, self-confident, willing to carry the team on their back, and believe they can fix all problems. The hero the school wants and needs.

As a style, 'leader as hero' has become very unfashionable. I have read articles that divide leadership into heroic and post-heroic periods. However, I don't think we should be sidelining any one leadership style. Indeed, I believe my leadership style has often been in the 'leader as hero' mode. In addition to cleaning out storerooms, I have led schools to *National Awards for Excellence* and *State Awards for Improvement*.

Note my use of '*has often been*'. There were times when I engaged in other styles – styles which better suited different situations. The key to understanding the 'right' leadership approach starts with the contradictions in the role and how they are influenced by context.

The Leadership Contradictions

There are contradictions inherent in what teachers, communities, and performance appraisals expect of school Principals, which will be expected of you:

- You will need to be flexible yet decisive, and, at the same time, cautious that flexibility isn't perceived as indecisiveness.

- You will be expected to distribute leadership, whilst accepting that the buck stops with you.

- You should be collaborative, seeking everybody's views, yet authoritative.

- You will be required to exercise judgement but sometimes to suspend judgement , allowing (some) situations to unfold.

- You will need to provide a safe, stable, secure environment but challenge the *status quo*.

- You will need to lead with your heart but have plenty of backbone.

- You will need emotional intelligence, but you'll also need to crunch the numbers.

In the fairy tale *Goldilocks and the Three Bears*, Goldilocks is presented with extremes in the temperature of the porridge. Eventually, she finds the one that is 'just right'–the middle bowl.

Underlying the fairy tale is the tension between extremes that is resolved through a middle ground compromise. Goldilocks found that the middle bowl was not too hot and not too cold. It was 'just right' for her.

This middle ground compromise might not always be the right solution. Context depending, school leaders might find that they need to take the hot bowl, pushing

> through change. They might need to get excited and enthusiastic, driving things forward. At other times it might require the cold bowl. The situation might need some careful and calculated planning. There are times to weigh in and there are times to lean back. Sometimes the situation will need 'leader as hero' (the hot bowl) and sometimes the situation will be better served by the servant-leader model (the cooler bowl).

As Goldilocks teaches us, it is better not to think in terms of having *a* leadership style, but to think in terms of finding the style which is *'just right'* for a given situation.

In my experience the role of school Principal can be exhilarating. It can also be exhausting. Perhaps it is to be expected, given the contradictions, that it will produce contrasting experiences – sometimes on the same day.

> **REFLECTION**
> **On Contradictions:** Are there any examples in your own work where you have faced the contradictions above? How did you reconcile them?
> **On Leadership Styles:** Do you have a default leadership style? Can you name it/describe it?

Three Leadership Roles

In addition to leadership styles, there are three roles that are relevant to our reimagining theme:

- Gatekeeper
- Cosmopolitan
- Maverick

You might find yourself in any one of these roles over the course of your time in leadership. Each of these roles can determine the nature and pace of reimagining in your school. Each has its strengths and its weaknesses.

The Gatekeepers

> *"Never chase after buses, attractive women, or new ideas in education. There's sure to be another one come along in about twenty minutes."*

I first heard that from a school Principal in 1976. It could come straight out of the '*Gatekeeper's Guide to the Universe*'. Gatekeepers decide what gets through their school's metaphorical (and literal) front gate and what doesn't. They decide the merit of new ideas.

Gatekeepers sift through new proposals and innovations to determine what is and isn't appropriate *before* there is any staff participation. They are the custodians of the rules and standards. They tend to embed themselves in their schools. They are the unsung heroes of isomorphy, of sameness. Gatekeepers are more likely to be found in schools driven by traditions. They have a strong tendency to keep the gate shut.

Gatekeepers are unlikely to have visionary plans—the *status quo* is the plan. They might even roll back innovations that have been introduced by a predecessor. Sometimes, it is part of their employment brief.

In the first chapter we looked at UNESCO's future scenarios for schools. The first scenario suggested schools would continue to muddle through with very little actual change. We are likely to find high numbers of Gatekeepers amongst the Principals of these schools. We might also find them leading the second scenario schools, the 'for profit' sector. A sector where owners expect careful husbanding of their investment, not a cavalier attitude to the use of their money.

Are you a Gatekeeper? Whatever your answer, there are times when you might need to be. If your school is in a crisis, or in some way overwhelmed, you might need to adopt a gatekeeper role to minimise the distractions and demands. Stability management is no less important than change management. Gatekeeping can clarify what is important, what is trendy, and what is necessity.

The Cosmopolitans

By contrast, Cosmopolitans are open to every idea.

Fullan writes that one of the most consistent attributes of successful Principals is that they have a 'cosmopolitan' outlook[3]. Many have worked outside education or travelled widely. Fullan believes this is an essential aspect of successful leadership. Gender, personal charisma, or extroversion are less important than being receptive to new ideas. The cosmopolitan Principals can be working in rural settings, the inner city, or the suburban fringes. It is their mindset that is cosmopolitan, not their geography.

I am a self-confessed Cosmopolitan. My cosmopolitan tendency is, in part, a result of working in international schools. My 'neuroplasticity' was thoroughly challenged when I began working in an environment where "Yes" might mean "No", or 2 pm meant 5 pm. Adapting to a new country, culture and climate can provide challenges that make us

---

3. Op cit, Fullan, p110

receptive to different and challenging ideas. Challenges which make us more cosmopolitan.

As 'my educated life' has taught me, Cosmopolitans are likely to have complex strategic plans as they (we) try to implement the 101 great ideas they (we) have encountered. It is necessary for Cosmopolitans to control this instinct. New ideas should be run through two simple tests; if the innovation fails either test, proceed with caution:

- Will it improve student outcomes?

- Is it sustainable?

The third of UNESCO's future predictions sees schools as 'Social Welfare Centres' and the fourth projects strong 'Learning Communities'. Each of these would suit the Cosmopolitan.

For some Principals, their world experience is narrow, constraining the cultivation of ideas-an accurate description of the Gatekeepers. To break free of this I encourage exposure to new concepts, new people, new cultures, and new contexts. Ask yourself: what are the sources of new ideas that you currently access? Is it through professional organisations, educational journals, a collegiate network, a course of study, a coach or mentor? Any of these can provide the stimulus you need to kick start a reimagining of your school-the catalyst to open the gates, to open *your* gates.

The Mavericks

The Mavericks don't police ideas like the Gatekeepers or embrace every idea like the Cosmopolitans. The Mavericks *create* ideas.

The Mavericks want to pull the future towards them. They tend to have an inclination for taking risks. They are serial reimaginers. Mavericks like to focus on the inspiration not the limitation. They want to do what's not been done before.

On the other hand, Mavericks often have little interest in turning their ideas into a coherent plan. And they have the potential to fall flat on their faces. A.S. Neil, B.F Skinner, and Ivan Illich from Chapter 2 are each great examples of mavericks. Each enjoyed success but also great disappointments. Neill's Summerhill faced bankruptcy, Skinner was accused of experimenting on his own children, and Illich's celebrity lifestyle was subjected to a Vatican Inquisition.

The Mavericks might find employment in UNESCO's second scenario – the 'for profit schools.' However, it's likely to be a tumultuous and short-lived employment. The Mavericks might also find a role in the fifth scenario, the deschooling option. There is a place for visionary entrepreneurs in that brave new world.

If that is you, a cautionary note: you can only adopt the Maverick role for brief periods. There are risks attached which can create chaos in a school. You could, however, use the Maverick persona to challenge a seriously moribund situation. Schools can easily slip into comas. It might take a Maverick to wake it from its slumber. But be aware that many people enjoy their sleep and might not welcome your interruption.

My Educated Life

> *Sydney, 2022*
>
> As Covid finally loosened its grip I made plans to sell my house in Sydney. It had been the family home for over sixty years. It was the place where my migrant family had put roots into Australia's soil. My parent's gradual transition from seeing England as 'home' to Australia 'being home' was realised inside its walls. That transition was completed by my daughters and grandsons who speak with a *'strine* accent and have skin baked brown by the southern sun.
>
> The sale completed, I sold or stored my possessions. I bought a one-way ticket to Saigon. My own leadership journey was behind me. My last Principalship a memory.
>
> Reflecting now, it had been an opportunity for me to be a cosmopolitan one last time, to bring some of the hero, and some of the servant. To open the gates for others.

As we've seen, school leadership is full of contradictions and complications. Understanding leadership styles, and which style might be *'just right'* for a given situation, helps. As does being able to move through different leadership personas: gatekeeper, cosmopolitan, maverick. The challenges will remain though. The raw material we work with are complex human beings. There are no easy solutions.

I was reminded of this fact some years ago when I offered to lend my copy of Fullan's *'New Meaning of Education'* to a colleague. He replied that he would read his first book on school leadership only when he finished reading the complete works of Shakespeare. These would contain all the lessons about human conceit and courage that he would need to manage a school. In retrospect, he was right. It's all there. The flawed rulers, the fateful decisions, the jealous underlings, the unexpected developments, and the selfless acts. As I've learnt on my own journey, from Sydney to Hoi An, as a school Principal you should expect your own share of dramas.

And it is to drama we now turn. In the two previous chapters we've considered 'the crisis in our schools', but what happens when a school faces an actual emergency? For the next chapter I will present some of my educated life's more dramatic episodes — I'll let you judge whether they are worthy of Shakespeare.

CRISIS

Dealing With The Things We Never Imagined

"When written in Chinese, the word 'crisis' is composed of two characters. One represents danger and the other represents opportunity."

John F Kennedy

Reimagining a school can create difficult and challenging situations. However, it is unlikely to cause an emergency.

An emergency is unpredicted. It is an event that we never imagined. The best we can do is have a plan which helps us to deal with these sudden and unwelcome events. A plan which supports a proactive, not a reactive response.

In this chapter I present five very different types of crises I experienced during my 'educated life'.

My Educated Life

Kyoto, Japan, December 2023

Kyoto was the capital of feudal Japan from 794 to 1868. It is the treasury of traditional Japanese culture and life. Our family holiday ticked a long-standing box on my 'To

> Do' list. I have been intrigued by Japan's art, poetry, and aesthetic for decades.
>
> The Japanese use the word 'ran' to describe a knot or whorl in a piece of timber. The ran interrupts the smooth flow of the grain. Before and after the ran the grain is uniform but inside, it is chaotic and full of the unexpected.
>
> The Japanese also use 'ran' to describe a crisis. The regular, expected flow of life is suddenly interrupted by chaos and upheaval.
>
> Once you are past the ran the smooth flow of the daily grain/grind resumes. The Japanese advise using that time to review what went well and what could have gone better. Too often these opportunities for reflection are missed when the press of the next day obscures our experience...until another 'ran' comes along and disrupts the smooth flow of the grain.

CRISES AND LEADERSHIP

The Bus has been Hijacked

My school in Papua New Guinea (PNG) operated a fleet of 15 buses. The first pickup started around 6am with teachers and their children. The senior staff had long held concerns for the safety of these early morning runs that ran close to settlements full of 'raskol' gangs.

And so it came to pass that one morning the bus from Hohola did not arrive at the expected time. The driver was not responding to the Operations Manager's calls. The bus had been hijacked. We sent another bus to the area with armed security guards on board. They found the staff by the side of the road. The driver had been attacked and had a head wound. One of the female teachers had been sexually assaulted in front of her children. Another female teacher had a broken arm. Every adult on the bus had been robbed of their money and phones. The bus had been taken. An emergency was unfolding with wounded and traumatised staff.

This was the day we never wanted to see.

My first action was to print out copies of our 'Critical Incident Protocol'–the plan that would guide us through this 'ran'. I convened a meeting of the senior staff. We revised the roles and responsibilities outlined in the plan.

Unsurprisingly, during a crisis people can react emotionally. It is human and understandable but emotional reactions are not what is needed. There was:

- A triage station to set up
- Wounds to be treated
- Transport to hospital to arrange
- Victims to be counselled
- Relatives to contact
- Police to notify
- Staff to reassure
- Classes without teachers
- Timetables to reschedule

- Unscheduled assemblies to organise
- Parents needing reassurance
- Newspaper reporters' questions to answer
- A Board of Governors to inform.

Fortunately, we had prepared for this kind of incident. The Critical Incident Plan laid out what should happen, who should do it, and when it should be done. We hoped never to have to use it, but were glad to have it when the day came.

I have talked with school leaders who reject the need for such a plan. It is a very optimistic outlook. An average size school will have an enrolment of around 350 students, a similar number of parents, and 40 to 50 staff. To imagine that the lives of these 700 people will run smoothly and safely over one to three to five years is naïve. The crisis may not be as extreme as a hijacking, but being prepared is critical nonetheless. I've known schools where: a student was fatally locked in a school bus; a heartbroken adolescent breached school security in search of the heartbreaker, intent on harm; a popular student died in a car accident two weeks before her final exams.

The schools that responded best were those with a Critical Incident Plan.

> **RELECTION**
> **On Critical Incident Plans:** Have you experienced a school crisis that did, or would have, benefited from a Critical Incident Plan?

The Library is on Fire!

It has been said that a crisis is also an opportunity. Words never truer than the night the Korobosea International School library burnt to the ground.

My PA rang me around 11pm to tell me of the disaster unfolding. By the time I arrived fire brigades were controlling the blaze. However, my PA and Deputy Principal were both in states of high anxiety. I was grateful that the fire had been contained and not spread across the campus, but they were in shock at the loss of this major asset.

The following day the charred remains of the old building smouldered with acrid smoke. It was a Sunday and many staff had come to survey the damage. Like my PA and Deputy, they were also deeply upset—many were in tears. For people living in a country as poor as PNG a library can be a symbol of many things. The knowledge it contains, the promise of learning, and hope for the future.

In truth the library was awful. It was a Dickensian place that I avoided. It was dark and full of ancient books. Most of the computers did not work. There had been no investment in the library for decades, but to the staff it was a valued asset. I needed to contain, even conceal, my personal view of the library as I consoled my staff.

The following week the school's accountant informed me that the building and its contents were fully insured. The new building would be a straightforward replacement. However, it was the content insurance that changed everything. The computers were written off with no value. The same for the furniture and equipment but the books—mouldy and irrelevant—the books were different. Books don't depreciate the way computers do. My attitude to those ancient tomes changed quickly. Magi the librarian had catalogued every book that had ever been purchased. The final calculation for the loss of the books was astonishing.

From a crisis came opportunity.

It was an opportunity for a reimagining. Should we replace the contents with a conventional library or was this a chance to reinvent? Could we maintain a fiction section but reduce, even eradicate, non-fiction in expectation that the internet would be a better source of information for the students of today and tomorrow? We invested heavily in desktops, laptops, Interactive Whiteboards, and *Kindles*. We put significant money into routers and wiring.

When the library opened we unveiled a facility the like of which the city and country had not seen before: students involved in online maths competitions with children in Mexico and Turkey; teachers demonstrating science experiments on IWBs; parents reading to their children from *Kindles*.

Miracles and wonders from grief and tears.

There were lessons to be learned from this crisis. The first is to understand that your staff can form emotional attachments to buildings, classrooms, and even equipment. These are attachments that we might not share but it is necessary that leaders recognise the attachments and the process of letting them go. They are symbolic to the person. A change of classroom might mean leaving a room that someone has spent many productive years in. The dropping of a welfare program might signal the end of an era to a staff member. We must be sensitive to these vulnerabilities. I might have thought that the Koro library was a liability but, to many of the staff, the library was a symbol of hope in a troubled country.

Every crisis has multiple points of view.

The library fire also demonstrated the need to be as calm as you can be in a bad situation. When a school is facing a tragedy or an emergency the school's leaders must project reassurance to the staff.

Oh, and make sure you have paid your insurance premiums.

> **REFLECTION**
> **On Crisis:** Do all crises provide opportunities?

Personal Crisis

What happens when you, the leader, are the crisis?

I have often told the staff at my schools that a day was coming when I would drive away for the final time. All I would leave behind was a legacy. The legacy I wanted to leave would be the capacity of the staff to maintain the school's integrity and purpose in my absence.

My time in PNG concluded sooner than I expected.

One evening I began to experience severe stomach pains that increased in intensity. I eventually phoned my PA who arrived a short time later to take me to hospital. I was diagnosed with advanced typhoid and spent the following week in ICU. My PA later told me that the doctor had given me a 50/50 chance of surviving. From my hospital bed, I fretted.

How would the school fare during my sudden and prolonged absence?

I need not have worried.

The Bursar, with thirty years' service, provided institutional memory. The Deputy Principal exercised the authority that a single mother with four children can command. The Operations Manager kept the buses running and the Stage Leaders ensured the teachers remained focused. All the leadership staff took some responsibility.

The lesson I took away from this episode was that the investment I made in capacity building (as covered in Chapter 7) yielded a priceless dividend.

My recovery was good. My appetite returned, requiring a visit to the local supermarket. As I drove into the roundabout in front of my compound, I was confronted by a group of men armed with machetes. They blocked the road and began attacking my car. The automatic door locking did its job initially, but with a man at each door using bush knives to pry open the door locks, I had little time and one choice. I began a U-Turn back into the traffic behind me. I escaped, but the word was out that the men perpetrating the hijacking had lost face and would be waiting. I moved into a friend's house, changed my car, and carried a personal alarm around my neck—it would trigger an armed SWAT team guaranteed to be at my location within five minutes of activation.

A friend even offered to sell me a gun...but a better friend told me:

"The day you think you need a gun is the day you should leave."

By the end of the year I had done just that.

> **REFLECTION**
> **On Absent Leaders:** What might happen if you, the leader, are absent from school for a day, a week, or a month? Who would step up? What gaps might be left unfilled?

Toxic Schools-Self Induced Crisis

The term 'toxic' has become popular to describe poor work environments. It is worth reflecting on how it is that schools become 'toxic' given that their primary role is nurturing.

A toxic school culture is defined as an environment where teachers do not trust each other, and where the mental health of the staff is impacted in a negative way. It is the result of poor behaviours and bad habits being left unchecked. This malevolence can be rooted in self-interest, self-promotion, or self-preservation.

At the individual level, it would be easy to call these traits those of an immature personality, but I have learnt that behind every selfish act lies an unresolved sense of injustice. Very often this sense of injustice goes unrecognised by the perpetrator–it simply lurks behind their decision making. Then, when enacted collectively, these behaviours become accepted as the norm—a norm that inevitably leads to a crisis.

It is critical then that we are alert and ready to recognise signs that our workplace is becoming toxic.

A specific example I experienced was the 'literacy wars' that dominated education in the 1990s. The issue divided the staffroom into 'whole language' and 'phonics' camps. People had strongly held views regarding the correct approach to the teaching of reading. This escalated into a 'progressives' and 'traditionalists' division. The situation then moved beyond pedagogy and became personal.

I failed to recognise this escalation. In doing so (or, rather, not doing so) I contributed to it.

Many teachers are very passionate about their pedagogy. Passion management is a challenging aspect of school leadership. Objectivity is often the first casualty. In the literacy wars we had gone beyond pedagogy and become a toxic staffroom with divided loyalties. Trust, hope and care were in short supply.

Recognising signs of the deterioration is not easy—much of it occurs away from the leader. One way to mitigate the effects of a toxic culture is to provide a Grievance Procedure. Such procedures can resolve issues before they escalate. Procedural fairness is necessary for it to be successful. There will be difficult conversations and possibly tears. However, nipping toxicity in the bud will save leaders a lot of disturbance and distraction later.

Eventually, through a combination of counselling, negotiation and a few hard conversations we managed to bring down the level of toxicity. One staff member did, however, elect to leave. She remained uncomfortable with some of her colleagues. It was a valuable lesson in the importance of maintaining vigilance in our relationships.

> **REFLECTION**
> **On Self-Induced Crisis:** Have you experienced a toxic staffroom? What was the cause? How was the situation resolved? How could it have been avoided?

The Dark Side of Leadership-A Crisis from the Depths

At a recent leadership conference, a presenter suggested that there were times when a Principal might need to 'go over to the dark side.' It was greeted with a ripple of recognition by those in the room. The presenter went on to warn that good managers should make sure that their stay on the dark side was brief and did not become a place regularly visited or one where permanent residence was taken.

What do we mean by '*the dark side*'?

Judy Smeed's review of the literature relating to the use of power in schools includes Blasé and Blasé's levelling of Principal's negative behaviour. It is disturbing reading:

- Level 1 has Principals discounting, isolating, and abandoning teachers.

- Level 2 involves spying and sabotaging.

- Level 3 Principals have escalated to serious aggression, lying, forcing teachers out of their jobs, harassment, and racism.[1]

It's enough to make you think that the collective noun for a group of Principals is—a 'lack'.

Over the course of my educated life, I have heard many stories of school leaders behaving badly—going over to '*the dark side*'. One concerned an inexperienced but ambitious Principal who systematically rid himself of the leadership

---

[1]. Smeed J 'Power Over, With and Through' Journal of ACEL, Vol 15, No 1, 2009, p28

team he inherited from his predecessor. The team was composed of capable and popular people. His justification was that he wanted his own team. The effect on the teaching staff was palpable. At a staff meeting one frustrated teacher openly stated:

"I'm ashamed to work here!"

It was the trigger for a crisis of confidence. This kind of crisis, created by ambition, does not recognise its potential to destabilise a school and can put years of reputational development in jeopardy.

> **REFLECTION**
> **On the Dark Side**: Have you ever travelled to the 'dark side'? Did you make it back?

One lesson that I learnt early in my career was that when you step into a role with power, you are no longer seen as an individual, but as a symbol of authority. How you use that authority will determine the culture of your school. Your performance will be amplified throughout the organisation. It can make people proud or ashamed to be part of it.

My Educated Life

Kyoto, Japan

The purpose of our brief visit to Kyoto was to see snow. It was a long-held desire of my wife who is from the humid central coast of Vietnam. Kyoto has ancient temples, bamboo forests and philosophers' paths, but my wife was only interested in one thing. Yet, after seven days of

> sightseeing with plenty of sunshine, there was no sign of snow.
>
> On our final night, the weather prediction was cold and dry. The following morning, as we packed to leave, we watched snow falling from our hotel window. If only life had the same predictability as weather forecasts. It doesn't, so be prepared and have a plan.

School leaders should expect a crisis at some point in their career. In this chapter we have looked at ways to limit the impact. In the next chapter we will look at how to limit the possibility of a critical event developing before our eyes.

SAFE SCHOOLS

"Safety is the most basic task for us all. Without a sense of safety, no growth can take place. Without safety all energy goes to defence"

Torey Hayes

One of the UNESCO future school scenarios covered in Chapter 2 is 'Schools as Well-Being Centres.'

This reimagining has its origins in the work of A.S. Neill and his Summerhill school. The primary purpose of these schools is the wellbeing of students. Academic progress is valued but is secondary to social and emotional stability. This stability is seen as a necessary precondition for learning and academic success. Safety, in its very broadest sense, is paramount.

There are many ways we can make our schools safe. Whole books have been written on the topic. Here I focus on four areas which I have found to be critical: duty of care, inclusion, bullying, and wellbeing. Each of these, if not managed correctly, has the potential to make a school unsafe. The chapter offers some advice on how you might ensure that is not the case.

My Educated Life

Hoi An, Vietnam, 2022-24

For most of its history Vietnam was divided into three kingdoms. In the north the Viet Kinh had a love-hate relationship with Imperial China. Confucianism was and continues to be a major influence. The south was dominated by the Buddhist empire of Angkor in Cambodia. Wedged between these two was the Hindu kingdom of the Cham. The Cham was a commercial empire that flourished from the 12th to 16th centuries. Its main trading post was Hoi An. Merchants from China, Japan, Portugal, and Malaysia built shophouses—the small city prospered.

Over time the river began to lose its depth due to siltation. The traders moved further north to present day Da Nang. Hoi An was lost in time until in 1995 a UN World Heritage listing returned it to the world's attention. Today Hoi An is a global destination. Each day thousands of tourists flood into the 'Old Town.'

Following COVID, the Vietnamese border reopened on March 15th, 2022. I reentered on March 20th.

I met my partner in Saigon after a separation of two years. We travelled to Hoi An, to our new home. We married after eight years of being 'partners'—a term she always disliked. I slipped further into the quiet of retirement.

SAFE SCHOOLS

Duty of Care

In 2001 I was given the task of introducing the staff at an Australian school to major legislative changes to the statutory 'Duty of Care'. With over a hundred staff, their values ranged widely. The changes were upsetting to some, challenging for others, and offended the sensibilities of a few.

One of the important issues to emerge from this presentation was the poor understanding many teachers had of the Duty of Care as it applies in schools. Throughout my 'educated life', this has too often been the case.

While there is a general Duty of Care between all citizens, in schools the standard of the Duty is heightened due to the presence of children. Children cannot be expected to predict danger to the extent that can reasonably be expected of an adult. Predictability is one of the key legal considerations in establishing negligence (i.e. fault).

Many teachers do not understand the implications of failing the Duty of Care. If a child is seriously injured due to negligence it is very likely to trigger a criminal investigation. Alternatively (and possibly also), the injury might lead to civil action by the parents of the child. They can seek compensation for the injury from the school and the teacher.

In 2019 three staff from an international school in Hanoi received jail sentences following the death of a student at their school. All three were found to have been criminally negligent in that they failed to follow the school's established procedures. The parents of the student also launched a civil suit against the school and were successful.

One of the major misunderstandings I have seen in schools exists around the waivers parents are asked to sign. These waivers seek to release schools from any responsibility for injuries suffered at the school and on excursions. Lawyers in Malaysia, Australia, and Papua New Guinea have advised me that these waivers are not worth the paper they are written on. Leaders and teachers need to understand that the Duty of Care they have to their students cannot be signed away. Teachers and schools cannot and should not seek to absolve themselves of responsibility for the safety of the children in their care. No waiver in the world will prevent a criminal investigation and charges of negligence. Proforma school waivers are easy to find on the internet, but that does not make them legal.

Some years ago, I took a group of students on a three-night excursion to Australia's capital, Canberra. We were sharing our motel with students from another school. I was supervising the students from my school. The children from the other school were becoming increasingly reckless. None of their teachers were supervising. I saw three girls walk out the main gate and disappear into the night. I went looking for their teachers and found them in the motel's bar. When I warned them of the girls leaving the grounds the lead teacher replied:

"It's OK. The parents signed a waiver."

This is a disturbing example of how waivers can create complacency among school staff. Some staff will engage in negligent behaviour in the mistaken belief that the waiver provides legal protection. It won't.

At each of my seven schools, one of my first acts for the new school year was a presentation on Duty of Care. This presentation was intended to reduce the chances of a serious injury on the campus. It also served to reduce (though not absolve) the school's legal liability. If an injury occurs due to negligence, this annual training can be used as evidence of the school acting responsibly. The teacher's liability however increases if training was provided but subsequently ignored.

In addition to annual presentations, I have always been out and about around the campus. I walked the corridors to check if there were unattended classrooms. I would spend time in the playground ensuring teachers were on duty. I would be at the front of the school in the morning and the afternoon. My presence was a reminder to the staff of the responsibilities they have.

In my experience, the reputational damage caused by a serious injury at a school is ample justification for this policing. It takes years to build a reputation, but it can be lost in minutes.

> **REFLECTION**
> **On Duty of Care:** Are you up to date with the legislation regarding Duty of Care in schools in the country in which you are working? What issues do you face in addressing negligence in your school?
> **On Waivers:** Does your school currently use waivers? Do you agree that waivers have the potential to create complacency?

Inclusion

Government data in Australia indicates a 40% increase in enrolments of students with a disability in mainstream schools. Inclusion of children with disabilities in mainstream classrooms is a vexed question. Consider these recent headlines:

> *'I am all for Inclusion – in principle'*
>
> *'Inclusion Can Be Harmful – Ofsted Chief Warns'*
>
> *'Can Private Schools Ever Be Inclusive?'*
>
> *'Inclined Against Inclusion'*

Enrolling students with disabilities should be encouraged (and in government schools may be legally required) but is not without its challenges – challenges I have encountered in each of my previous schools.

The application for enrolment by a deaf girl in Malaysia, an autistic boy in PNG, a child with cerebral palsy in Indonesia and a sight impaired adolescent in Australia presented different but similar challenges. As the leader you must consider if your school really has the capacity to provide for these students' needs. If the answer is '*No*' then to maintain your school's integrity, you must consider denying the enrolment. Accepting the enrolment of a disabled child when you know that your school cannot cater for their needs is dishonest or worse – just another full fee. The decision might not sit easily with you. It might make you feel less than noble. It will certainly involve difficult conversations with parents. In those difficult conversations you might be presenting what you feel is in the child's best interest, but the parents are only hearing 'discrimination.'

Faced with this dilemma, in one instance, I agreed to a trial enrolment to "*see how it goes*". A deaf child was placed with a teacher who had no experience or training with children with hearing loss. This arrangement produced a lot of frustration for the teacher—with themselves, but also with the child. The teacher's frustrations were predictable. She was required to adjust classroom routines, academic programs, and behaviour management to ensure the inclusion was successful. This required additional preparation. There was further work after the lesson to document the steps taken and the adjustments made. These are significant additional requirements and, understandably, they were resented. The result was a far less than ideal learning environment for the student.

The initial parent enrolment interview had been tense, but nothing compared to the interview where I informed the parents that the trial was unsuccessful, and that the enrolment could not continue.

As the person ultimately responsible for enrolments, it is our duty to provide additional support and training for the teachers involved. We might feel we have been inclusive about the enrolment, but we cannot then place the burden on the teacher and hope that it all works out. It almost certainly won't.

As the school leader you might need to make the right decision, even when it feels all wrong. My advice is to consult broadly to generate a policy that is clear and public. If a situation arises, refer to the policy.

Bullying

Over the last decade 'bullying' has become a term used far too easily and far too frequently.

It seems that there has been a global outbreak of bullying. Small frictions between students too easily become claims of bullying. Parents arrive at the Principal's office demanding action, incensed by the 'bullying' their child was subjected to. Let's be clear: bullying does occur. It is amongst the most serious discipline breaches a student can commit, but bullying has specific criteria. People in leadership need to ensure that the criteria is met before we convict. We devalue the experience of those who are suffering from genuine bullying by conceding to lazy definitions.

The criteria that I apply before determining if bullying has occurred, includes:

- A power imbalance exists between victim and perpetrator—physical or social.

- A repeated occurrence—it is not a one-off incident.

- The bullying behaviour is kept secret, often occurring purposely out of sight in unsupervised areas (i.e. it isn't just roughhousing, tomfoolery, or playfulness which gets out of hand).

An example comes from my school in Kuala Lumpur. Two boys were part of a football game. At the end of the game there was a scuffle; one boy was pushed to the ground. Words were exchanged. The duty teacher intervened. Was this bullying? Does it meet the criteria above? Probably not. There may have been a physical power imbalance, but football is a contact sport. It was in the open, in the moment, and most likely a one-off. It was not acceptable behaviour and resulted in disciplinary action, but it was not bullying. When the parent of the boy knocked over arrived in my office incensed by her son being 'bullied', I needed to stand my ground. It did not meet the criteria and it would be an injustice to label the other boy a bully—he was in the wrong, but he wasn't guilty of bullying.

Unfortunately, too many parents and students are invoking 'bullying' with no real understanding of what bullying actually is or the effect that such accusations can have on other students.

In my experience your stance will be fortified if an investigation has already been conducted into the incident, before the parent's complaint. It is even better if you are proactive and inform the parent of the incident in advance of the child arriving home. The most important aspect of any investigation will be the provision of procedural fairness, particularly for the student accused of bullying. Procedural fairness ensures that both sides of the story are told. To deny procedural fairness to a student risks sowing the seeds of resentment and retribution.

> **REFLECTION**
> **On Bullying:** Does your school have a policy on bullying? Were students involved in drafting the policy? Have there been claims of bullying in your school? How were they addressed?
> Are your bullies shown alternative ways to behave? Are punitive measures appropriate for students determined to be bullies? Or is it an emotional wellbeing issue?

Wellbeing

In late 2023 a Facebook post took my educated life in a surprising direction, back into classroom teaching. Back to where it all began.

I began working as a substitute teacher covering absences at a local international school. This school places a strong emphasis on the wellbeing of its students. Most of its public messaging demonstrates this commitment. It is an emphasis that is gathering momentum across the world with schools from many different backgrounds making student wellbeing their priority. They project the image of safe hands in an increasingly unsafe world.

Schools are receiving ample support for this new attitude. I recently received an invitation to a World Education Summit. The summit offered nine online courses. Four of the topics were related to wellbeing including: The Age of Identity; Ferocious Warmth; Inclusion and Disability; and Engagement and Wellbeing. Only one workshop was dedicated to improving pedagogy.

I have seen thousands of graduating students. My experience leads me to suggest that there is one common 'wellbeing' characteristic. It is confidence. Not all the graduates were extroverts. Some had a quiet assurance, but each had the confidence to:

- Speak in front of others
- Express their values
- Undertake high stake exams
- Try new things
- Form relationships
- Socialise comfortably
- Learn from their mistakes.

There are many valuable characteristics that schools can develop including patience, compassion, flexibility, and kindness. All are aspects of wellbeing. However, each of these needs a confident personality to find expression.

We have thirteen years to preserve and build our students' confidence, but confidence can easily be lost. In my experience the primary threat to confidence is exclusion. A sense of exclusion, of being different, usually results in loneliness. Loneliness is the health equivalent of fifteen cigarettes a day.

The erosion of confidence starts with a student developing that sense of being different. They hear:

- You're not like us;
- We don't want you on our team;
- Your results aren't up to standard;
- You aren't invited;
- You're weird.

Schools and teachers prioritising wellbeing need to make the development of confidence their first topic of conversation. Whether they are neurodiverse, LGBTQ+, or just introverted, your students' chances of successfully negotiating the world, with all its prejudices, will depend on confidence.

My Educated Life

Hoi An, Vietnam

It is the week before Tet, the traditional New Year in Vietnam. As the week progresses the traffic and markets become more frenetic. Men are hustling for money to appear prosperous. Women are harried by the dozens

> of jobs still to be done. Everything must be cleaned. Gym instructors are wiping down equipment and bank employees are cleaning ATMs.
>
> Hoi An is a small place but on any day a deluge of tourists pour through its streets. Retiring to a global destination has many advantages. There are international cuisines to taste, beaches to surf, rivers for kayaking. And time to sit down, listen to good music, and, from the comfort of my new home, reflect on my educated life. The world continues to change and our fortunes change with it. Hoi An, once the centre of an empire but then forgotten by time, is once again vibrant and evolving.

Schools need to be safe places—that's a given, a foundation, a starting point. As school leaders, we are the people with the primary responsibility for making this happen.

We need to set a high bar for the Duty of Care. We need to regularly remind staff of their obligations and be proactive in our policing. We need to be inclusive; we need to do the right thing, but the right thing may be making hard decisions about whether your school is the right one for a given child. We need to guard against bullying, and guard against easy indictments of bullying. We need to promote and protect the wellbeing of students, starting by focusing on the development of confidence.

Only when our schools are safe can we feel confident about change, confident about a reimagining. In the next chapter we look at a key driver of change—technology.

SCHOOLS AND TECHNOLOGY

"It is not about the machine, but about the possibility."

David Warlick

As we saw in Chapter 10, some educators are calling for student wellbeing to become the primary purpose of schooling. Technology presents a significant obstacle to this purpose. The mental health concerns being raised around technology are hard to align with wellbeing. Research from the U.S. National Library of Medicine claims that smartphone dependence causes sleep deprivation, anxiety, and negative self-imaging. It even has a name—*nomophobia*—the fear of being without your phone[1].

Such concerns aren't new. In 1930 a group of mothers known as the 'Scarsdale Moms' convinced the US National Broadcaster's Association to create a code of conduct for youth programs that would:

---

1. Abi-Jouade E (2020) '*Smartphones, Social Media, and Youth Mental Health*', National Library of Medicine, v192

"refrain from glorifying greed, selfishness, and disrespect for authority."[2]

It seems quaint today, but this was to counter the insidious influence of radio on their children. Yes, radio.

My Educated Life

Bangkok, 2024

Earlier this year my wife and I decided, on impulse, to have a weekend break in Bangkok. Our visit coincided with Songkran, a major Thai religious festival. Traditionally, water is sprinkled on people to symbolically wash away misfortune. These days it is a hedonistic carnival—it has been taken to extremes. To control the situation, the Thai government has banned high powered water guns, powder smearing, foam parties, and sales of alcoholic beverages. Necessary steps because sometimes we all take things too far.

Controlling our impulsive natures is a story as old as the Bible, the Gitas, and the Analects. Songkran has become an unregulated playground where strangers and children can interact freely—what could go wrong?

A not very subtle segue to technology, students, and schools.

---

2. Cross A (2018) *'What Kind of Tech Scared Parents in the 1930s?'* Journal of Musical Things

Fast forward to the 1960s and there was a similar parental alarm that the introduction of colour television was affecting the eyesight of children. It was colonising their leisure time. Worse still, it was affecting their moral compasses.

Today, parental fear is focused on social media. An example comes from Canada where four school boards are in a $4 billion legal action against *Meta* and *Tik Tok*. They claim that the sites are disrupting student learning. The school boards argue that the platforms:

> 'are designed for compulsive use and have rewired the way children think, behave and learn'.[3]

It seems that technology has a long and continuing history of frightening parents – and teachers.

Prohibition and control are popular solutions but teenage impulsiveness, whether having to own the latest tech or ranking classmates by looks, is not easily controlled.

School leaders are right in the middle of this fight.

Should we be initiating bans and prohibitions? Actions that always seem to end up on the wrong side of history. Should we be embracing technology, going all in? And yet, as explored below, there are legitimate concerns that children's mental health is being adversely affected by these devices.

> **REFLECTION**
> **On Concerns:** Has technology changed the brains of twenty-first century children? If you are a parent, have you placed time restrictions on your child's internet use? How's that working out for you...and for them?

Schools and IT: A Brief History

In the decade from 1997 my school, like most others, purchased multiple desktop computers to demonstrate that we were keeping up with 'Information Technology.' We created 'computer labs' to take us to the twenty-first century. Next, we put laptops on trolleys and began rolling them in and out of classrooms. Around 2004 we introduced Interactive Whiteboards (IWBs). We established an IT department. It all seemed necessary and responsible.

It also came at a very high cost. And it was not only the machines. The infrastructure and maintenance added to the expenditure. Our newly created IT department was trying to keep it all running. If a printer didn't print, a laptop stopped working, the Wi-Fi went down, or all the other things that could go wrong went wrong, you called the IT department. This became financially (and emotionally) unsustainable for schools. Enter Bring Your Own Device (BYOD).

At the time BYOD seemed the perfect solution. The devices the students brought to school reflected their interests, and capabilities. If there was a problem with the device it was the student's problem. The students initially brought laptops and tablets. There was still a lot of excitement and—yes, innocence—surrounding this infiltration into schools.

Before too long laptops and tablets became passé, uncool. Teachers were soon waging a battle against mobile phones.

One survey of a school district in Virginia found that about a third of teachers were telling students to put away their cell phones five to ten times per class, and 15% did so more than twenty times a class. 75% of respondents thought that cell phones were negatively affecting their students' physical and mental health. Nearly two-thirds believed the devices were adversely affecting academic performance.

From around 2017 schools began banning phones in schools. The justification for this drastic action included the levels of addiction, classroom disruptions, cyber-bullying, sleep disturbance, and the easy access to pornography. BYOD was no longer the solution but a big part of the problem. Exit BYOD.

Were the IWBs, desktops, laptops, and tablets all a big and expensive mistake?

The introduction of the technology created a lot of excitement and engagement, but did it improve students' academic performance? A 2015 OECD report concluded probably not:

> "In countries where it is less common for students to use the Internet at school, students' performance in reading improved more rapidly than in countries where such use is more common."[4]

Three places regularly cited as examples of academic success are Singapore, Shanghai, and Finland. According to the OECD report these countries' schools have only an

---

4. OECD 2015 'Students, Computers and Learning'

'average' expenditure on IT. Their success is a result of their investment in pedagogy, not IT. Conversely countries that have invested heavily in IT including the UK, US, and Australia have not seen significant improvements in their national testing results.[5]

John Hattie's 2013 meta-analyses of computer-assisted instruction found that:

"...the net effect may be zero."[6]

We might ask if the money could have been better spent on hiring additional teachers, providing PD or, better still, increasing teachers' salaries.

Cautionary Tech Tales

The brief history of IT provides two cautionary tales for school leaders. The first is the push to adopt technology. The second concerns the introduction of technology, only to have to withdraw it.

The first caution is to avoid jumping on the latest bandwagon. From 1996 to 1998, print and television were saturated with reports about 'IT'—an extraordinary new set of technologies that would change, well, everything. It was difficult not to be caught up in the gravitational pull of this future. History is full of examples of people rushing to be part of the latest big thing. Common sense is often an early

---

5. Ibid, P148

6. Ibid, P163

casualty. It's hard to be the only lemming saying: "I think I'll sit this one out."

An example is provided by the 'Reading Machines' that were introduced to schools in the 1970s. The machine would project a text onto a screen. A cursor would then follow the text word-by-word. Students followed the cursor to read the text. These were expensive acquisitions, but many schools had two or three. Research then revealed that the eye does not track in the linear manner of the reading machine. The eye jumps ahead of the word being read — sometimes two to three lines below. It 'grabs' words from further in the text. The reading machines were put back into their boxes and are probably still sitting on shelves in cupboards in forgotten storerooms.

The second cautionary tale is the roll out and, in many schools, subsequent roll back of BYOD. It is not a good look for any enterprise to implement a change only to reverse the decision. The roll out of BYOD as a solution to the rising cost of maintaining IT was sensible at the time. The eventual roll back recognised that it had created different problems and a string of unintended consequences. True, predicting how an initiative might play out is not easy, and factors beyond our control often determine the course of events, but make the wrong calls too often, and confidence in leadership is affected.

The lesson from these cautionary tales is straightforward: have a good understanding of what you are introducing before you introduce it. Whether it's a different form of assessment or a change to your executive structure, or a roll out of new technology. Take time to work through and talk through the implications. Ensure you are acting with clarity and not responding to hype. History is riddled with sober people making regrettable decisions.

> **REFECTION**
> **On Thinking Through**: Have you introduced or seen the introduction of an initiative which created new problems? How do you think this can be avoided?
> **On AI**: How will you determine which of the coming AI initiatives will be beneficial?

The Alphas and Their Tech

Generation Alpha, children born after 2010 (and before 2025), have known only a digital world. Since birth they have been immersed in social networks, and streaming services. IT has provided them with soothing distractions, intriguing images, and humiliating messages – all through an addictive delivery system.

Whether this technology is a blessing or a burden is a question that their parents, teachers, and governments are grappling with. On any day you can read that someone, somewhere, has called for smartphones to be banned or for social media to be controlled. Academic Jonathon Haidt has addressed the issue in his best-selling book, 'Generation Anxiety.' Haidt unequivocally blames the use of smartphones for:

> "...creating the tidal wave of adolescent mental illness ."[7]

---

7. Berrocosso, J. (2022) *'Educational Technology and Student Performance'*, Frontiers in Education

Critics argue that Haidt oversimplifies the issue. They do not dispute the surge in adolescent mental health disorders but argue that there are more significant causes, particularly Covid. A meta-analysis of 40 published research articles by Odgers found no causal relationship between social media usage and mental health.[8]

However, Gen A's use of technology is pervasive. According to the Pew Research Centre about one third of 13 to 17 year-olds use social media 'almost constantly.'[9]

This brings us back to impulse control. These devices have opened the door to an unregulated space where strangers and children can mix freely. A space where the worst of human excess can flourish: bullying, trolling, liking, ghosting, following, deep faking, phishing, and click-baiting.

As we saw above, we've been here before. The printing press, radio, TV, the internet, and now social media have all challenged parents and teachers. Undoubtedly though, technology has accelerated the pace at which we are presented with these problems. Anyone involved in school leadership in the last 30 years, perhaps even the last 100 years, has been trying to find solutions.

Prohibitions are rarely effective. Negotiation is usually better than enforcement. We need to provide avenues for consultation, particularly with students.

The issue of mobile phones and social media in schools is far from resolved. Combined, they exemplify every school leader's dilemma—caution and progress. We need to avoid

---

8. Ibid

9. *'How Teens Navigated Covid'* 2/6/22, Pew Research Centre

rushing to adopt the 'latest' but can't afford to ignore the trends. Roll outs and retreats come at a cost in dollars and confidence. Will you be a '*Gatekeeper*' or a '*Cosmopolitan*' (Chapter 8)?

My Educated Life

> *Hoi An*
>
> Over the last few nights my wife has begun taking her iPhone into the bathroom. She listens to podcasts during her evening shower. When I asked why she had this sudden need she replied: "It's boring." I was tempted to ask her how she had coped for the previous fifty-two years of monotonous ablutions but refrained – no one likes a smart...alec. It does raise the question of how she acquired this sudden need for distraction. Did the technology meet an unrecognised need or did the technology create the need?
>
> The unregulated use of technology, especially the internet, is a playground for excess and there are a lot of children playing there. Even responsible adults are being seduced by it. Even my wife. How to control a beast that feeds our impulsiveness is a challenge not only for schools and Gen A but for our whole civilization.

What is the lesson here then? It is that we must commit to technology, but we must also be cautious.

How can you recognise that you might be rushing in when you should be holding back? How can we know when expenditure might not produce the expected benefits?

I suggest you ask yourself:

1. Will it improve student outcomes? And, how do you know?

2. Is it sustainable, financially? Long after the excitement wears off, will it still be a good idea? Will staff and students still be motivated by it?

Today, school leaders must be scanning the future with some trepidation. If mobile phones can cause this amount of disruption, what havoc will AI inflict on their schools? Time and yet more tech will tell.

REIMAGINING SCHOOLS - REVISTED

"The future is in the decisions we make now".

Ishita Gupta

Bringing my educated life and this book full circle, in this chapter we return to the UNESCO report from Chapter 2. In that chapter we looked back thirty years, to the influencers who shaped the predicted scenarios. Now, we consider how prescient the report has been.

What does it have to say about the present? About the future? About your possible future?

My Educated Life

Time Travel

To stave off the groundhog days of retirement I recently sorted through my chest of travel mementos. I came across a menu from 1977, my first international flight. Even in the cheap seats, it was in full colour and offered a range of course options. The menu is from a time when travel was still a luxury. The flight took me to Bali and the start of the overland 'hippie trail' that would eventually lead me to London. I would see the slopes of Everest and riverside cremations in Varanasi. I would drink mint tea in Kabul, observe the curfew in Tehran, marvel at Istanbul, and be scammed in Penang.

International travel isn't what it used to be. It used to be glamorous. Now all the style and taste has disappeared behind the walls of exclusive corporate lounges and into first-class seats. A situation some might suggest is being repeated in education.

Schools were never glamorous, but they aren't what they used to be. In many countries students are disappearing into the expensive seats of fee-paying schools. Unlike the airlines though, luckily for today's students, this does not mean that quality is restricted to these schools. Over the course of my educated life, I have worked in Catholic, Jewish, Anglican, Islamic, community, government, not-for-profit, for-profit, and international schools. In each of these settings, I have seen conscientious teachers provide excellent education for students from many different backgrounds—rich and poor. Mostly, these teachers were motivated by a love of the job, regardless of where the money was coming from and how much of it there was.

I want to do a little time travel. I want to cast forward from UNESCO's 2000 report. How prescient was it? Can it (still) predict the future many years after its publication? Can it provide some guidance to a new generation of school leaders? Can it help guide you?

The UNESCO Future Schools Scenarios

Making predictions risks embarrassment. By the time you read this there might well be evidence which proves my predictions naïve or misguided. What I offer then are only possibilities. A range of things that might come to pass during your educated life.

Let's recall the six scenarios:

- In Scenario 1 schools continue to muddle through with increasing stakeholder dissatisfaction.

- Scenario 2 sees the expansion of for-profit schools, including as commercial arms of large corporations.

- In Scenario 3 schools become centres for wellbeing.

- In Scenario 4 schools become vibrant learning communities.

- Scenario 5 sees schools slowly dissipate to be replaced by learning networks which do not need specific physical settings, teachers, or timetables.

- In the 6th Scenario teacher scarcity causes widespread school closures.

Scenario 1: More of the Same

In this first scenario it was predicted that schools would continue to muddle through with more problems than solutions; they continue to resist reform due to embedded bureaucracy. Sadly, much of this rings true today. You probably know of schools finding themselves 'stuck', often because of governmental directives, pressures, or paperwork.

This scenario accepts that some of the tasks schools perform are necessary but not always 'educationally' orientated. For example:

- Socialisation and maturation of children into young adults.

- Supply of a workforce, which may not mean an educated workforce.

- Providing a protected space for children while parents are at work.

To meet these needs governments will continue funding schools, but with little effort to fundamentally change them. It might seem difficult to find reasons for optimism in this scenario. The lack of flexibility will inhibit initiatives. The absence of any systemic progress will affect morale. Teachers will leave the profession. Situations all too familiar to many of us today.

School leaders in this scenario must support teachers who are working to rise above the system's limitations. It requires leadership that engages with and advocates for teachers. Leaders will need to provide protection and support; even when frustration with the situation becomes dissatisfaction with the school leadership—as it will. The challenge, your challenge, if you find yourself in this scenario, is to create a culture of mutual support and trust; a sense of collective purpose to care for the children in front of you despite the systemic challenges facing the schools and children around you. To do the best you can with what you've got.

My experience in the government sector was brief, but I was fortunate to join a school led by a dynamic Principal. She knew how to extricate herself and the school from problems. She knew how to work around the limitations. She knew which edicts could be ignored and which couldn't. She secured resources, additional funding, and the staff she wanted. She knew how to be political. For me it was a lesson that change, and progress, can still occur despite system constraints. I saw how to 'play the system'. It's a lesson I encourage you to learn as well.

> **REFLECTION**
> **On Bureaucracies:** Will bureaucracies ever be able to balance accountability and autonomy? How will bureaucracies stem the exodus of teachers?

Scenario 2: Schools as Profit Centres

Scenario 2 suggests a very different model.

Two countries are illustrative of this scenario. Since 2009 the number of 'international' schools in Vietnam has increased 42%[1]. They are all 'for profit'. In Australia 36% of students attend private schools and 60%[2] of all new students are enrolling in private education. In both countries the increases are the result of parental dissatisfaction with state education. It is possible that the enrolment numbers in non-government schools will eventually match the numbers in government schools.

Of all the scenarios, the shift to for-profit schooling presents us with the greatest extremes: schools with strong corporate

---

1. Adams R (2023) '*Record Numbers of Teachers Quitting the Profession*', The Guardian, 8/6/23

2. McPherson, Emily (2024) '*Thousands of Australian Teachers*', 7News.com.aus, 27/06/2024

identity, for better and for worse; schools run as businesses, for better and for worse; and schools which value education, hopefully for the better.

Vietnam provides an example of the first possibility. One of the most popular choices for private education is the *Vinschool* chain. With close to 50,000 students enrolled across the country it has captured a sizeable slice of the market and continues to expand. *Vinschools* are only part of a vast conglomerate. You can live in a *Vin-Home*, drive a *Vin-Fast* car, shop in a *Vin-com* mall, holiday at a *Vin-Pearl* resort, and get surgery in a *Vin-Med* hospital.

The *Vin* example demonstrates that as companies become more confident in the educational space, schools that are part of conglomerates will develop corporate identities. Staff will be expected to respect the values of the company, values which might not necessarily align with those of teachers. Leadership is likely to be centralised, as are policies, procedures, and curriculum. Staff will be required to dress in corporate uniforms, including the Principal. This is the world of *McSchooling*; a future where education is subsumed to conglomerate goals.

A second possibility is schools with enlightened owners who are committed to education, to innovation, and to development. They will be willing to invest to be the best. With a competent 'Cosmopolitan' at the helm (Chapter 8), these schools have the potential to be fulfilling workplaces. For-profit schools have a commercial imperative to address concerns, to improve services, and to be proactive. It makes good commercial sense. On the downside, corporations with cultures of excellence, continuous improvement goals, and a 'good to great' mentality can be very demanding. They might not perceive that producing cars or vacuum cleaners is any different to producing school graduates.

The third possibility is schools where profit alone drives the culture. My own experience in these schools was disturbing. There was a high turnover of staff. Recruitment was at times desperate, resulting in the appointment of inexperienced and unqualified teachers. There was very little investment in resources.

So, what can you take away from this scenario?

Firstly, whichever version of these schools you encounter, there is one commonality—the relationship with parents. The parents and school have a contract. Fee paying parents are not averse to legal action if they believe the agreed service was not provided. As a school leader, managing this relationship might be one of your more consuming challenges.

Secondly, if you are looking at a position in this sector, do your research. Try to read between the lines of school websites, especially those owned by corporate groups. Read online reviews posted by previous teachers. Use the interview to probe the school's real values; try to get beyond the platitudes to the real motivations. If you can determine the culture of the school, carefully consider if it is for you. It will be a business culture. Review any contract carefully—corporations have formidable legal capabilities.

> **REFLECTION**
> **On Schools as Profit Centres:** How can Principals negotiate an increase in resources when every increase reduces profit levels?

Scenario 3: Schools as Centres for Wellbeing

The first two scenarios were unsettling. Here, thankfully, schools are reimagined to a different purpose. This is a sector that has seen significant growth. Many of these schools are 'not for profit.'

In this scenario the focus is on the 'whole child.' It takes us back to Chapter 2 and the alternative school movement. AS Neill's Summerhill placed students' emotional wellbeing and rights above all other considerations. The belief was that academic progress would follow if the socio-emotional domain was settled. It can be seen in The Royal Children's Hospital of Melbourne's recent statement:

> "We suggest shifting the core purpose of schools from primarily focusing on academic intelligence to focusing on wellbeing, and health...We need to co-create a new purpose for school education and not be limited to test scores and exam results. To give more students better reasons to come to school and perceive it as their happy place."[3]

However, for a growing number of students the socio-emotional domain is far from settled.

> "...a recent survey in the US of over 96,000 students found that levels of anxiety are

---

3. *'Re-inventing Schools'* Centre for Community Child Health Royal Children's Hospital of Melbourne

> increasing. The survey revealed a 21% increase in anxiety and a 17% increase in depression amongst teenagers between 2021 and 2022."[4]

In these schools, as you may have already experienced, leaders find themselves spending a lot of time explaining to parents the rationale behind holistic education. This is even more necessary in Asian markets where parents often have 'traditional' expectations. For leaders, these conversations are about reducing parental pressure on students, allowing them to find their own passions. Sure, honest conversations like this might not result in an enrolment but, if your context allows you to stick to your values, it is better to have clarification now rather than confrontation later.

For some this scenario will be wholly familiar and wholly welcome. For others it is anathema to why they teach. With wellbeing (in the broadest sense of its meaning) given primacy, time in these schools may be monopolised by sporting fixtures, drama performances, clubs, expeditions, charity work, and social action initiatives. These become the school's raison d'être. Time in classrooms is reduced. Teachers used to 'teaching' will need to adjust to this new role - to being a coach, mentor, and therapist - to being an educator of the 'whole child'.

Teachers uncomfortable in this scenario might ponder the implications if academic progress loses its primacy in schools. They might ask what happens when knowledge and skills are reduced? For some, it might mean letting go of some aspects of schools they value, even cherish. Moreover, if a characteristic of these schools is reducing the 'pressure' on

---

4. *'Students' Anxiety, Depression Higher Than Ever'*, Michigan News University of Michigan, 9/3/23

students how might this affect assessment and reporting? If the school does not want to pressure its students, how can it, in good conscience, engage in judgement and ranking? Should it? Do schools need to?

If you are considering a position in one of these schools, there are questions you'll need to ask yourself. Where do you sit on these debates? In Chapter 2 I outlined my decade of working in an alternative school. I have always valued academics yet, in this context, there were instances when my qualifications were perceived as an obstruction. At one meeting when I cited my qualifications to support an argument, a parent observed:

> *"Yes, you've been trained. Woof, woof."*

My years of dedication to academia were seen as an impediment to 'progress'. Ouch.

> **REFLECTION**
> **On Schools as Centres for Wellbeing:** Where does progress stop, and indulgence start? How will student behaviour be managed?
> Would it concern you if your science teacher skips 'Reproduction' using the time to discuss LGBTQ rights?

Scenario 4: Schools as Learning Communities

I have been the Principal of schools that made genuine progress towards becoming learning communities. The most successful achieved a high level of shared learning through a self-directed professional development program (Chapter 7). To my mind, learning communities are the finest expression of schooling. They are a statement of values and idealism.

They require flatter management and increased teamwork. They are high-trust rather than high-control environments.

However, there are aspects of learning communities that might not sit comfortably with some staff and governing bodies. Self-directed learning, capacity-building (Chapter 7), and distributed leadership are important components of learning communities, but they can also be interpreted as threats. Some school faculties are like silos, they will resist any attempt to change them. Some teachers see their classrooms as their kingdoms. Some school Boards feel it is their duty to maintain the status quo. These are all legitimate concerns and a reminder that schools are sites of contesting values.

It raises the question:

"How far would you be willing to go to defend the values you believe in?"

At the start of my career, I had successive appointments to Catholic and Jewish schools. Both the appointments were made by female Principals who were inspiring and progressive leaders. Each had created positive learning cultures. Unbeknown to me, both women had resigned and been replaced by the time I took up the positions. They both resigned on principle, unhappy with the direction their superiors wanted to take the schools. In both instances men were appointed to take over. They were recruited to roll back their predecessors' initiatives. Even as the newest staff member, I felt disappointment and anger as these deconstructions proceeded. It had taken years to build these learning communities, but they were gone within months. The schools went back to basics. Walls were rebuilt, teams disbanded, and rote learning reinstated. It was a statement of a very different set of values.

Those two women knew the hills they were prepared to die on. As the leader of a school do you know which hills you'll die on? Would this be one? Have you decided what's worth fighting for?

> **REFLECTION**
> **On Learning Communities:** Are 'not-for-profit' schools the best fit for learning communities? What values guide your decision making?

Scenario 5: Schools De-Schooled

In Scenario 5 schools slowly dissipate to be replaced by learning networks which do not require a physical setting. Learners work from whatever location they feel comfortable. This can be in a public library, or on a park bench. Learners utilise the internet, and human contacts to pursue their education in their own time and at their own pace. This scenario has its roots in another 'influencer' from the 1960s – Ivan Illich and his *'Deschooling Society'.*

This scenario is being realised today by thousands of students. These students are 'homeschooling', a convenience to avoid the legalities of compulsory schooling. They create their own program of study. Maths might be through the online Kahn Academy, science through Australia's Crest program, and English with a private tutor. They might also meet with their swimming coach three times a week and provide a few hours of community service at the local aged care facility. And when ready, they can sit whatever exams they prefer – UK, US, Australian, or others – as a private student.

There are over 40,000 children being home schooled in Australia. Many are neurodiverse, disabled, or school phobic.

Their families are creating online communities, arranging learning experiences, and developing education plans.

While it might seem that this scenario has little relevance to you, it is important for school leaders to understand the withdrawal of students in favour of homeschooling. Personally, it is a choice I would respect. I know families where homeschooling has been a great success. The flipside of this are the students who re-enrol after homeschooling. Many are school phobic; they stayed at home because school is intimidating. Schools enrolling these students will need to understand the extent of their fear and how re-entry will be a process of small steps, some forward and some backwards.

This scenario is a reminder to school leaders that there are levels of dissatisfaction powerful enough for parents to quit their jobs, reduce their incomes, just to keep their children out of schools. And these are just the ones who can afford it.

> **REFLECTION**
> **On Schools De-Schooled:** How much flexibility do you have in your context to address parental dissatisfaction before it results in disengagement and potentially homeschooling?
>
> Do we have an obligation to students after they leave? And how able are you to work with these families if they seek to return?

Scenario 6: No Schools

Scenario 6 comes about through an exodus of teachers that leads to the 'meltdown' of school systems. It is a dysfunctional reimagining that is currently being played out just as it was forecast many years ago. For example:

- The world needs 44 million more teachers if education is to be provided to every child.

- In Australia 9% of primary school teachers quit the profession in 2022, almost double the rate of 4.6% in 2015. And, more than 13,000 schools have closed in central and west Africa over the past four years.[5]

We need to consider the possibility that schools will cease to exist in many parts of the world. Compulsory schooling has been part of human history for less than two hundred years–a blip in the human journey that is measured in hundreds of thousands of years. Schools might well be consigned to the past in many parts of the world. This will have global and local effects.

At the global level the closure of schools in the developing world will further entrench social inequalities. The vacuum created by this absence will be a fertile place for political and religious radicalisation. It has the potential to destabilise nations and put international trade and stability at risk. In Chapter 7, I cited the example of Cambodia under the Khmer Rouge and their elimination of schools. It did not go well for the Cambodians, but it also destabilised the region.

There are many schools in the developed world already struggling to staff their schools. The predicted surge of resignations and retirements means that your school will face increasing competition for staff. You will be forced to offer better incentives to secure staff to remain viable. A situation that is likely to favour fee-paying schools.

---

5. McPherson Emily (2024) *'Thousands of Australian Teachers'*, 9News.com.aum, 27/06/2024

I imagine you may well already be experiencing some of these pressures.

> **REFLECTION**
> **On the Meltdown:** How can we stop teachers leaving the profession and encourage new ones to join?
>
> Beyond money, what new incentives could you provide to recruit and retain teachers?

Beyond UNESCO - Yuval Noah Harari and a New Species

A different reimagining to those included in the UNESCO report is provided by the influential academic Yuval Noah Harari.

Harari has predicted that we are "*very near the end of our species.*" Harari is not predicting a nuclear annihilation but a transformation. He believes that humans in a hundred years will be as different to us as we became to Neanderthals. The human beings of the future will be transformed through interfaces with AI. Their bodies will have different abilities. Their minds will operate with different capacities. As I sat down to write this morning, CNN presented the story of a paralysed man who can control a computer with his thoughts—no wires attached. The technology behind it is called Brain Computer Interface. The implications of this for schools and education are profound.

Harari's prediction is bold. If it does come to pass, it will change human nature and in turn, education. It would require a reimagining of what it means to be human and what it means to be a teacher. How will schools adapt to educating a different species of humans? Will there even be schools? Or knowledge and skill 'upgrades' as downloads?

What we can say is that AI will have a profound effect on schools and society. More immediately though, how will it affect the delivery of the curriculum? How will it affect the emotional stability of students? If the predictions that AI could cause the loss of 300 million human jobs are accurate, how will it affect the validity of the school-to-employment pathway? What becomes the point of school (as defined and experienced today)? Who knows? Right now, no one.

My Educated Life

Time Travel

I first heard Talking Heads' song 'Once in a Lifetime' in 1980. It has remained a favourite. More than a few times I have recalled the opening verse:

And you may find yourself in another part of the world
And you may find yourself behind the wheel of a large automobile
And you may find yourself in a beautiful house, with a beautiful wife
And you may ask yourself, "Well, how did I get here?

Most of us, at some point, ask ourselves "Well, how did I get here?" Perhaps, with the emphasis on a different word in the sentence each time we ask ourselves the question.

How did I get a beautiful house, with a beautiful wife, on the central coast of Vietnam?

> My educated life is an accumulation of school appointments. Some lasted decades, others just a year. It began in a remote valley in Australia, moved to the Indonesian archipelago, onto the wilds of Papua New Guinea, then to the cities of Malaysia, and finally to this house in Vietnam. In between there was travel across the globe.
>
> There was no rhyme or reason, no strategic career plan. It might be an example of fortune favouring the brave. Apart from the two years tied to a 'for-profit' school, I recall all the appointments without regret. I once read that when faced with choices, the most radical of the choices will lead to the greatest growth. My educated life in a nutshell.

Conclusion

Courtesy of UNESCO, we have some sense about the future of education—where it is potentially heading. Did you recognise your school amongst the scenarios?

- Are you 'working the system' in the 'more of the same' scenario?

- Are you in a school that is only one part of a much bigger commercial enterprise?

- Are you readjusting to a school where academics are a secondary concern?

- Are you building a learning community?

Whatever your own context, in the short-term, we will probably see more 'more of the same' schools. In the medium-term, corporations are likely to have more influence over education. Longer term, tragically, there will be more parts of the world without schools.

You and I have very little capacity to affect those futures. However, we can influence schools where learning communities or wellbeing are embedded in their vision. When I reflect on my educated life, travelling back in time in my mind, it is these schools I enjoyed the most. It was in these schools that I feel students gained the most. And it is to these schools I would encourage you to apply. Schools where you can cultivate or preserve their foundational values. Schools built on **hope**, **trust** and **care**.

AND IN THE END
Lessons From A Life Lived in Education

"Bruda, makim skul gudpla."

Babani Maraga

Let's begin the ending by casting back to the 17th of February, 1870 and the passing of the United Kingdom's Elementary Education Act. The act that made school attendance compulsory.

The following day a government official arrives at the house of a farmer to inform the family that, starting tomorrow, the children must report to the new building in town—a building with a disturbing similarity to a prison. They will be put in the care of complete strangers. These strangers will have authority to discipline the children as they see fit. The children will spend the day being instructed in knowledge and skills with no relevance to farming. The official tells the parents it is compulsory. Failure to comply will result in legal actioneven the removal of the children from their home. This is not for a day, he tells them, it is for the rest of their childhood and adolescence. At the end of this time, the children will be processed and their value to society determined. Parents are banned from entering the site. Starting tomorrow they must entrust their precious children to strangers.

How would the father respond? Would he emit a protective growl? Would the mother gather the children closer to her? Does this all sound far too melodramatic?

If it does, you have not witnessed the first day of pre-school anywhere around the world. Children cling desperately to their mothers as complete strangers try to pry them loose. The anguish of the mothers is manifest in their tears. Fathers encourage their sons to be brave. There is a lot of crying. Teachers become complicit. We tell the parents:

"Just go, she'll be OK...once you leave."

We, complete strangers, the teachers, restrain the child as parents shake their heads and hurry to the school's exit. Inside the classrooms, the unforgiving accumulation of expectations begins. Expectations that will govern behaviour, communication, and learning for the next 13 years.

Schools are artificial constructs. They are completely different to humankind's historic arrangements for education. For centuries an aunty, a cousin, or a brother taught the skills and knowledge necessary for continuity. Compulsory, comprehensive schooling tore those arrangements apart. The state assumed the power to define and control education. Education would serve industrial development and national identity. It created a monolith.

The monolith was characterised by uniformity and conformity. It stood unchallenged for a hundred years. Then, as we've seen, the great influencers—Neill, Illich, Vygotsky and Holt—created cracks in the monolith. They disrupted how schools were imagined.

Building on the work of these visionaries, we've explored how teachers and Principals began exploiting the cracks with their own reimaginings, great and small. Schools, your schools, have created partnerships with families. Parents are now inside: as volunteers for reading, learning support, library, and sports; they are on school councils. Schools hold 'open days.' Corporal punishment is prohibited. In some schools, you can even learn about farming. And, if you prefer to learn at home, that can be arranged. The farmer and his family from 1870 would be amazed at the diversity of schools available to them—and at how different schools are.

"Bruda, Makim Skul Gudpla"

My time in school leadership, 'my educated life,' took me from the working-class suburbs of Sydney to a remote Australian valley, to the edge of the Indonesian archipelago, to an elite Anglican school, from the grinding poverty of Port Moresby to the uber-wealth of Kuala Lumpur, and eventually to an ancient town in Vietnam.

I was fortunate to work in schools that allowed me to realise the reimaginings presented in this book. Reimaginings based on trust, care, and hope. Reimaginings that sought to understand the subjective experience of change. Reimaginings that balanced support and accountability. Reimaginings that provided self-direction. Reimaginings of leadership.

I secured leadership positions because Board members and school owners saw something in me. They saw someone they felt they could trust but, equally important, someone who brought hope.

At the end of my first Board meeting in PNG an elderly member held my hand and said in creole:

"Bruda, makim skul gudpla." (Brother, make the school better)

The expectation that I would improve schools is a commonality to all my appointments. It is their hope. It is their permission to reimagine – to take some risks.

Perhaps you have already begun your leadership journey or perhaps it is an aspiration. Either way, a desire to learn about leadership is likely your reason for reading this book. I thank you for investing your time (and money) in it. My hope is that it has provided some directions, some solace and some wisdom. Given the challenges of the work there will be times when you will need all three.

The Final Contradiction

Successful leadership is a balance between change and stability, between being a *Gatekeeper* and being a *Cosmopolitan*.

The number of books on 'Change Management' can be measured by the tonne. It is a subject that has dominated school leadership for decades. Some change is necessary, and some is inevitable. I will bang the drum one last time – successfully implementing change requires an understanding of the subjective experience of those expected to change. You must know and understand the lived experience of teachers, students, parents, and of yourself.

A lot less has been written about 'Stability Management' but we must provide the conditions people need to be productive. They need predictability, a sense of meaning, and they need consistency.

Change management and stability management are not necessarily oppositional. Despite their apparent contradiction they can be complementary. A stable environment provides the best platform to launch a change. Change management and stability management are two sides of the same coin. They are both necessary for successful school reform. They require leaders who have the wisdom to reconcile their contradictions; leaders willing to learn lessons from their own educated lives.

I will leave you with some of my own learnings; wisdom distilled from thirty-five years of school leadership:

Build trust

Be willing to take risks – it creates hope

Care for and about people

Cultivate relationships

Develop your understanding of change

Provide support and accountability

Listen more than you talk

Learn to work with the contradictions of leadership

And, above all:

Never stop reimagining

Other Titles From

PEDAGOGUE Publishing:

International Schooling: The Teacher's Guide

The Wisdom of Heads: short advice for school leaders

Avaliable wherever you get your books from, print or ebook.

www.ingramcontent.com/pod-product-compliance
Lightning Source LLC
Chambersburg PA
CBHW030301100526
44590CB00012B/471